HUBRIS

HUBRIS

WHY ECONOMISTS FAILED TO PREDICT THE CRISIS AND HOW TO AVOID THE NEXT ONE

MEGHNAD DESAI

YALE UNIVERSITY PRESS
NEW HAVEN AND LONDON

For information about this and other Yale University Press publications, please
contact:
U.S. Office: sales.press@yale.edu   www.yalebooks.com
Europe Office: sales@yaleup.co.uk   www.yalebooks.co.uk

Typeset in Arno Pro by IDSUK (DataConnection) Ltd
Printed in the United States of America.

Library of Congress Control Number: 2015933801

ISBN 978-0-300-21354-6

A catalogue record for this book is available from the British Library.

10 9 8 7 6 5 4 3 2 1

CONTENTS

FIGURES

PREFACE

In July 2007, I was invited by the Ministry of External Affairs, Government of India to give a talk to a group of Foreign Services Officers on the prospects for the global economy. The group consisted of 150 people of a variety of ages and included ambassadors and senior diplomats. The discussion quickly turned to the global boom and I was asked by a senior diplomat from Brazil whether this boom would last. Over the course of my many years within the field of economics, I have learnt that there are two things that are certain; the longer a boom lasts, the more people buy into the idea that it will carry on forever and, secondly, the longer the boom, the greater the likelihood it will end soon. But economics is not an exact science so I could not give the diplomat a precise date for when the boom would end; just the certainty that a turning point would come and it would be sooner than he thought.

By mid-2007, two events had taken place, in quick succession, which indicated that the global economy was changing direction. The first occurred in the autumn of 2006 when the US housing market bubble burst; this was followed by the collapse on the Shanghai stock market in February 2007. These events were, at the time, viewed as isolated incidents, unconnected to the larger web of the global economy. During the Great Moderation, words like capitalism and business cycles were no longer a part of the vocabulary of modern economics used by self-respecting economics departments. Perhaps because of this, when the crisis finally hit, its severity took some time to register. Just as in World War I, belligerent nations expected the troops to be home within four months, by Christmas, many economists took the view that the crisis was temporary and self-correcting. Others said that while the crisis was serious, we had the means to solve the problem. The first batch were the New Classicals and the second Keynesians. My own view was that this recession was not only one of the deepest we had ever seen, but also that the usual Keynesian remedies would not work.

In February 2009, as the British Prime Minister Gordon Brown was proposing a massive internationally coordinated Keynesian reflation package at the G20 summit in London, I wrote an article for the online edition of a major UK newspaper about the perils of following a Keynesian policy solution.[1] It was clear to me that the cure would not come from a repetition of the old policies of borrowing and reflation. Globalization had fundamentally changed the context. To find a solution to the crisis we needed to explore the "underworld," as Keynes described it, the world where economists who had gone out of fashion lived. Karl Marx, Joseph Schumpeter, Nikolai Kondratieff, Friedrich Hayek (and even Knut Wicksell, who was still read but not understood) viewed capitalism as a system which was subject to the waves of up and down cycles – as a dynamic disequilibrium system. Modern economics views the market as a stationary equilibrium system – where decisions taken are compatible, so in essence supply equals demand.

When he came to office in January 2009, Barack Obama understood that the financial collapse had created a problem for the real economy. He launched a program for reviving the economy of nearly $800 billion which would have been right for a "normal" recession. Six months later, Alistair Darling, the British Chancellor of the Exchequer, became the first senior politician to recognize that the severity of the crisis was unprecedented. British elections were imminent by the autumn; along with my colleagues in the House of Lords, we were discussing what should go in the Labour Party's manifesto. I recall venturing that there was no money for any spending initiatives. The contest was going to be about whether Labour could do austerity better than the Conservatives. The answer came from above

---

[1] Meghnad Desai, "Keynesianism Isn't Working," *Guardian*, Feb. 16, 2009.

that we were not talking of austerity but of investment and growth.

Undaunted, in February 2010, along with a group of 19 other economists I signed a letter to the *Sunday Times* saying that, whichever party came to power, its government would have to cut the budget deficit within one Parliament. Among my fellow signatories were my colleagues at the London School of Economics Tim Besley and Christopher Pissarides (Nobel Prize 2012), David Newbery from the University of Cambridge, Tom Sargent from New York University (Nobel Prize 2011), Ken Rogoff from Harvard, and others. I was the sole signatory who had a political affiliation. There were two contrary responses in the form of letters to newspapers from my Keynesian friends Lord Richard Layard and Lord Robert Skidelsky, with many, many, more signatures for each. In the United States Paul Krugman was arguing strongly for a massive fiscal boost, while the New Classical economists of Chicago and Minnesota were skeptical of the need for, or the effectiveness of, any stimulus. Only among the central bankers of the United States and the United Kingdom was there agreement that the money supply had to be boosted by quantitative easing.

Four years later and with hindsight, we can see that the crisis was severe – one of the deepest ever. We also know that the recovery is fragile, at best, in the UK and the US, and non-existent in the eurozone. With the possibility that the recovery may be destabilized by the slightest wrong turn, now is an opportune time to reflect on what went wrong. The problem was not so much with the economy but more importantly with economics and economists. I want to address some of the questions that have been raised about economics: why economists failed to predict the crisis, what happened, why it happened when it did, and why economists won't admit that they were wrong. I also want to address the criticisms of the overuse of mathematics in economics and to see whether there is a new economics which can cope with future economic catastrophes better.

I write as someone who has lived through and even participated in the changes in economics that I describe herein. During my 50-plus years as an economist, I was a Keynesian while a student and in the first decades of my career. I battled against monetarism, writing articles and a book. But I also explored political economy in the works of Marx, Schumpeter, and Hayek through my entire career as an economist. As time went on, I witnessed the change in the culture of academic economics. It abandoned empirical habits of studying the economic reality and became wedded to aprioristic reasoning which replaced skeptical inquiry. Uncertainty and doubt were replaced by certainty and hubris. I tried my best to resist it. I continued trying to interpret the world anew in light of events with the tools of empirical research combined with a deep grounding in the heritage of economic theory. It continues to be an unfinished task. It is this change that I wish to bring home here. I hope readers will gain some insight from reading this book.

ACKNOWLEDGEMENTS

I must mention Robert Skidelsky for many close encounters over coffee and claret in the Bishop's Bar in the House of Lords where we discussed many of the themes of this book. A chance meeting on a train with Vernon Bogdanor gave me encouragement to finish what I had begun as a long note to myself. David Marsh read an early version and directed me to Yale where Taiba Batoul read the manuscript and told me how to make an ugly duckling into a better looking duck though not quite the swan she would have liked.

To all my hearty thanks.

INTRODUCTION
Unraveling the Threads

The Great Recession has been the deepest since the Great Depression of the 1930s. For the vast majority of people this has been the biggest economic upset of their lives. They may have heard stories about the Great Depression – the advent of Hoovervilles in the US and the hunger marches in the UK – but their lives have been spent in more comfortable circumstances.

The trigger was a financial crisis that quickly spread through the economies of the Western world with debilitating consequences. The events that began with the decline of the housing market in the US and climaxed in the bankruptcy of Lehman Brothers resulted in a set of circumstances which fits the definition of a financial crisis:

A sharp, brief, ultracyclical deterioration of all or most of a group of financial indicators – short-term interest rates, asset (stock, real estate, land) prices, commercial insolvencies and failures of financial institutions.[1]

This initial shock was followed by the loss of output and of jobs, which is now being called the Great Recession. Across the Western world there have been certain similar developments. The effects of the recession continue to be felt five years on. Although the global economy has now started to show the signs of a recovery, it will be many years before economic indicators return to precrisis levels. This was a crisis which was largely unanticipated by economists, financiers, and policy-makers and it has prompted questions about why it happened and how it was allowed to happen, since even as the economies of the US and UK are beginning a fragile recovery, there is still a lot of misery in the eurozone and Japan.

What Happened?

August 15, 2007 was a significant day. Apart from being the sixtieth anniversary of Indian independence, it was also the thirty-sixth anniversary of the day on which President Richard Nixon announced that the US would renege on its obligation to buy gold at $35 an ounce. That obligation had been the foundation of the postwar system of exchange rates known as the Bretton Woods system. It was named after the town in New

Hampshire where in July 1944 the Allies had met and hammered out the postwar order for international monetary relations. The Bretton Woods system kept all exchange rates fixed in relation to the dollar, while the dollar was fixed in terms of gold. This was the Dollar Exchange Standard. It replaced the Gold Standard that had been around for 300 years prior to World War II. Nixon's rejection of the obligation to buy gold at a fixed price ushered in an era of flexible exchange rates. It gave birth to the world we know today with changing exchange rates and easy conversion from one currency to another.

This time, August 15 was to be a memorable day for Timothy Geithner. The 46-year-old Chairman of the New York Federal Reserve Authority had begun his working life as a career civil servant at the US Treasury. He had dealt with currency crises and capital flight abroad and at home, including Mexico in 1994 and the Asian crisis of 1997 involving Thailand, Indonesia, South Korea, and Malaysia. He had no experience of banking. Nevertheless, in 2003 he was chosen to be the Chairman of the New York Fed. As the financial center of the US, if not the world, New York attracted the best players in financial markets, boasted some very big banks and brokerages, and presented a challenge even to the most seasoned central banker. To be the Chairman of the New York Fed was a big step up for Geithner.

On that day, Countrywide Financial – the largest subprime mortgage lender in the US with two decades of solid growth behind it – found itself short of the necessary funds to meet its liability payments. Mortgages were big business. Countrywide was not the only big firm dealing in mortgages. House prices had been rising for a decade and everyone expected them to go on rising. The borrowers were mostly creditworthy but during the Clinton Administration a deliberate attempt had been made to extend mortgages to households that would not otherwise qualify. They had fragile income and employment records. They were buying their houses in the hope that as the house prices rose their debts would become payable, while interest rates would remain low. Household debt, which had been steady at around 45 percent of household income between 1965 and 1985, had risen to a peak of just under 100 percent by 2007. Much of this was mortgage debt. Lenders such as Countrywide would loan out the money for mortgages and borrow in turn from short-term money markets against the collateral of these mortgages.

At the other end of the globe, China had been growing at double-digit rates. Its voracious appetite for raw materials put pressure on the commodity markets, where prices began to rise. For governments around the world this hinted at the possibility of higher rates of inflation to come. Consequently, the Fed changed its stance of holding interest rates low and hiked them up to 5 percent. House prices stopped rising. Countrywide faced sharply higher rates in the short-term market while the value of its assets – its mortgages portfolio – was being written down. Within a month, the price of insuring against its default had risen eightfold. It soon faced bankruptcy. On August 15, Countrywide approached Geithner and the Fed to bail it out.[2] But the Fed was reluctant. It first tried to get other banks to help Countrywide, whose equity price had begun to plummet. Eventually the Bank of America bought it out.

The contagion spread across the Atlantic. In September 2007 the British bank Northern Rock requested financial assistance from the government. The story is much the same. The bank had loaned out excessively in mortgages. It had securitized them and sold them on the international markets. Once the US market for subprime securities started to cool, Northern Rock became concerned that it did not have sufficient liquidity to refund customer deposits if they were demanded. Northern Rock initially tried to borrow money on the wholesale money market, but found it too expensive. As rumors circulated that Northern Rock was in trouble, depositors queued up to withdraw their money. The UK government had to rush to the rescue and nationalize the bank. Northern Rock was not the only UK bank to experience trouble, but it was the first UK bank to experience a bank run in over a century.

The crisis deepened in March 2008 when the 80-year-old American investment bank Bear Stearns also found itself in trouble. It had exposed itself in the securitized mortgage market and as the prices fell, its exposure increased and the Fed could not rescue it. It had assets of $400 billion but a debt of $33 per each dollar of its capital. Bear Stearns had already fired its CEO in January. It had to be sold at the low price of $10 per share compared to its recent peak of $133 to JPMorgan Chase, another US bank. This was followed by the collapse of Lehman Brothers in September of that same year: the fourth largest investment firm in the US went bankrupt after the US government refused to bail it out. Soon the collapse was general and AIG, an insurance firm, had to be rescued. US taxpayers had to put up $800 billion to launch the Troubled Assets Recovery Program (TARP). Geithner ended up as Treasury Secretary to President Obama, working through the aftermath of the TARP. Similar rescue programs were designed in the UK when the Royal Bank of Scotland, Halifax Bank of Scotland and Lloyds TSB all had to be rescued by the UK government through recapitalization programs – the buying up of a large proportion of bank shares, 86 percent in case of RBS.

A separate chapter of the Recession began in March 2010, when Greece experienced problems servicing government debt which stood at 150 percent; the norm would dictate 40 percent. It was also experiencing problems in tackling its large budget deficit (11 percent of GDP while the eurozone norm is 3 percent). Greece is a member along with 17 other countries of the eurozone. The eurozone is a single currency area with no federal government to supervise it and only a Central Bank – the European Central Bank (ECB), whose mandate is to deliver low inflation. This involves refraining from bailing out governments which have debt to sell. The contagion effect of Greece spread to Portugal, Ireland, Italy and Spain.

The slowdown in economic activity that began in 2007 and worsened in 2008 has cost the Western economies a huge loss of output. There are, as yet, no signs that there will be a recovery back to the "normal" precrisis levels of steady growth, full employment and low inflation. Since 2010, the eurozone economies' problems originating from Portugal, Italy, Ireland, Greece and Spain (PIIGS) have further depressed the course of incomes, employment and growth. They face a crisis of sovereign debt and have to contend with austerity as well as dealing with threats to their banks from shortages of capital and liquidity. Yet again special funds have been created to rescue banks if they get into trouble and the ECB has been helping out by supplying emergency liquidity.

Why Was It Not Anticipated?

In the midst of the crisis, Her Majesty Queen Elizabeth II on a visit to open a new building at the London School of Economics asked the now famous question:

Why did nobody notice it?

Professor Luis Garicano, the young economist tasked with replying, explained that everyone did what they were meant to do. It was no one person's fault. A group of economists who later wrote to the Queen called it a "failure of collective imagination of many bright people." There was "a psychology of denial," they added. So it was, and that goes a little way to answering her query. But as to what happened, why it did and why no one saw what was coming, the reply she got could not have satisfied her.

Since then some economists such as Nouriel Roubini have claimed that they predicted the crisis. But if this is the case, no one took them seriously. Raghuram Rajan, formerly Chief Economist at the International Monetary Fund (IMF) and the current Governor of the Reserve Bank of India, is credited with having argued, in 2005, that the new set of financial innovations were increasing the volatility in financial markets and heightening risk.[3] He was dismissed as a "luddite." Once the crisis struck, people recalled that the Bank of International Settlements (BIS) and the IMF had made gentle warning noises. The noises had to be gentle because of the fear that acknowledging the problem could make it a self-fulfilling prophecy.

An Economic Crisis or a Crisis of Economics?

Economics as a profession had been riding high in the eyes of the world. Economists were said to have the answers to all sorts of problems. Before the crisis, economic bestsellers such as *Freakonomics* (2005) showcased the power of economics to solve many social as well as economic problems. Alan Greenspan, former Chairman of the Federal Reserve, in his memoirs *The Age of Turbulence* drew a picture of a superman figure dominating the economy to whose charge he was appointed. Indeed many people in public life and most citizens believed economists had the tools to prevent events such as the Great Depression of the 1930s from reoccurring. All one can claim for economics is that our current predicament is not called the Great Depression but merely the Great Recession. I wonder if that is sufficient consolation.

Those few who understand economics, and the mindset of economists, said the failure to identify the crisis could be attributed to modern mainstream macroeconomics. This was because it had ruled out the possibility that such things could happen. Macroeconomic models are highly mathematical and are built around the assumption that markets always clear. In essence, that supply always equals demand and a balance – an equilibrium point – is reached. This precludes the possibility of a recession. Later, proponents of the black art said, in their defense, that such "extreme" events were by their nature unpredictable. Had anyone foreseen a crisis they could have profited from it and hence made the occurrence of the crisis less likely.

Robert Lucas, the doyen of modern macroeconomics and a Nobel Prize winner (1995), said,

One thing we are not going to have, now or ever, is a set of models that forecasts sudden falls in the value of financial assets, like the declines that followed the failure of Lehman Brothers in September. This is nothing new. It has been known for more than forty years and is one of the main implications of Eugene Fama's "efficient-market hypothesis" (EMH) which states that the price of a financial asset reflects all relevant, generally available information. If an economist had a formula that could reliably forecast crises a week in advance, say, then that formula would become part of generally available information and prices would fall a week earlier.[4]

The discussion has since moved on to what to do about the Great Recession. Economists have, broadly, split into two groups, those who call themselves Keynesians and those who are orthodox (mainstream). Keynesians say that the orthodox economists have forgotten the lessons John Maynard Keynes taught in his great work *The General Theory of Employment, Interest and Money*, which was written during the Great Depression. It argued that economies can get out of kilter, they can fall from full employment and get trapped in an underemployment equilibrium. In such an event, the answer is for the government to borrow money and spend it on job creation. This spending would be multiplied as people spent the money that had been borrowed and their spending would create more jobs in shops, factories, etc. The multiplier process would generate enough extra income to justify the initial borrowing. Keynesian economists cannot understand why governments are not grasping the initiative and borrowing money to get their economies out of recession.

The orthodox mainstream economists whose models failed to predict the recession say that the economy is always in equilibrium. Whichever level of employment the economy generates is an equilibrium one since the independent decisions of consumers and producers have brought it about. The Recession is a sign that there has been some "shock" – an unexpected event

– which has displaced the economy to a new lower equilibrium. The free market will get the economy back up as and when it does. People's actions are always taken in full awareness of the opportunities and costs of each action (rational expectations) and the sum total of their actions – demand and supply – always balances out to produce whatever is the case. They add that there will be no change in outcome if governments borrow money and spend it. This is because the taxpayers know that public borrowing today means higher taxes in the future to pay the debt back so they don't spend the money but save it for the day when taxes will have to be paid. Thus borrowing cancels itself out as far as any stimulus to the economy is concerned – this is known as the Ricardian Equivalence.

But others who advise governments have taken a more nuanced line. They say that borrowing and spending would not be the answer because it is the borrowing done in the years before 2007 and not since which has led to the current recession. Borrowing when the economy is doing well creates a structural deficit. Borrowing during a recession can, perhaps, be justified. That deficit may disappear when the economy starts growing again (Ricardian Equivalence being ignored for the while). But if you borrow when there is full employment, that deficit does not disappear. It remains on the government's balance sheets and becomes structural, leading to a deterioration in the GDP to debt ratio.

They blame the recession on excess government borrowing. They add that households also borrowed during prosperous times and incurred large, unsustainable debts. So borrowing

11

more at this stage would exacerbate the problem. Those who buy the government debt – pension funds, investment banks – watch the signals given by the rating companies which grade the quality of the government debt as triple A (the best and safest) down to triple C and so on. Borrowing when you are already in debt may lead to downgrading and then a higher interest charge has to be paid on the borrowing, making it costly.

Thus, while at the popular level economics seems to be going through a crisis, economists have not changed their ways of thinking. While some economists urge abandonment of the fancy models and going back to the older theories of Keynes with a policy of greater public spending, the bulk of the economics profession in the best universities is as smug as ever. The award of the Nobel (actually the Royal Bank of Sweden) Prize in Economics in recent years is a clue to how unshaken the profession is in its self image. Thus in 2013 the Nobel Prize was given to Eugene Fama (Chicago), Lars Peter Hansen (Chicago) and Robert Shiller (Yale). Only Shiller is at all unorthodox, though a fully paid member of the mathematical macro-modeling club. Thomas Sargent (formerly Minnesota now New York University) and Christopher Sims (Princeton) received the Prize in 2011 and both are original contributors to the "new classical economics" paradigm which is thought to have been discredited by the recession. Paul Krugman received the Prize in 2008 for his contribution to international trade theory not for his defense of Keynesian policies. The economics profession and its admirers, as the Nobel Committee must be, have not denounced modern economics as useless or as in some profound crisis. Who is right – the Prize givers and receivers, or the general public which is dubious of economics and economists?

Beyond the mainstream there are many pockets of unfashionable economics or heterodoxies, as we may call them. The economic theories of Marx have a bearing on the cycles, as do those of Frederick Hayek. who has his devoted supporters.[5] Economists such as Joseph Schumpeter or Nikolai Kondratieff were also much concerned with finding cyclical patterns in economic data over the two previous centuries. It is these economists who have more to say about how and why we are in the state we are in than mainstream or even Keynesian theories.

The Role of Globalization

As we are going through a crunch in the West, many economies in Asia, Latin America and Africa – the so-called "emerging economies" of China, India, Brazil, Indonesia and Nigeria – are debating "problems" of maintaining their growth at 5 percent or 8 percent or even 10 percent. What are they doing right that we are not? Could it be that what we had for three-quarters of a century – guaranteed prosperity and rising living standards – are about to disappear and become the experience of these countries who have been stuck in misery for the same long period? As they emerge, are we submerging? Is this the consequence of what is called globalization?

Globalization became a buzzword in the 1990s sometime after the fall of the Berlin Wall. It opened up an era of freer capital movements and freer trade across the world. It is hard to remember now that between 1992 and 2007 the developed and emerging economies enjoyed an unprecedentedly long period of growth with low inflation. These good things were attributed to globalization just as much as it is being blamed for the present slump. This was the period economists call the Great Moderation as quarrels among them about how the economy worked ceased after 30 years of debate (of course, they have resumed now). Mervyn (now Lord) King, the former Governor of the Bank of England, looked forward in 2005 to the years ahead of non-inflationary continuous expansion (NICE). How did that era end so suddenly? To understand the current crisis, we need to explore why the good times lasted so long and why they ended.

Where to Next?

There is no doubt that we are going through an experience which has had no precedent in the life of anyone born since 1945. But although this may sound like new territory, we have been here before. In the nineteenth century Lord Overstone described the pattern of cycles and crises as "quiescence, improvement, growing confidence, prosperity, excitement, overtrading, convulsion, pressure, stagnation, and distress, ending again in quiescence."[6]

Are we going through the down phase of this cycle and will we come up again? Should we be looking to past experiences for answers since our present resembles the Great Depression of the 1930s, or perhaps to even earlier crises? Does the solution to sustainable recovery lie in theories and approaches that have been relegated to the annals of economic history?

To find the answers we have to understand why economists think the way they do and how this thinking resulted in the failure to predict the coming crisis. We need to distinguish between two contrasting visions of the working of the economy. One views it as a static system almost always in equilibrium and never likely to suffer huge losses of output. The other views it as a dynamic disequilibrium which works by restlessly going through cycles of boom and bust, some of short duration while others last for decades. The two visions have coexisted in economics for a long time; the static vision has triumphed in academic circles while the other vision lives on in the marketplace and in the imagination of political movements. The latest crisis is a reminder that we cannot neglect the dynamic disequilibrium vision any longer. We need it to grasp the significance of what happened and what may yet recur.

PART ONE

Chapter One

THE BUILDING BLOCKS

Economics was born in a whirlwind of change. For centuries while the Roman Empire declined, Western Europe was caught in a stagnant feudal world with an unchanging cycle of poverty, misery, superstition and oppression. Year in and year out, life remained the same as if going around in a circular trap – same prices, same goods, same jobs, same short lives. The modern era which began with Christopher Columbus finding the Americas and Vasco Da Gama the Indies changed the economies of Western Europe. Spanish conquistadores brought large hoards of gold and silver from the New World. Between 1500 and 1700, 300 tons of gold and 33,000 tons of silver were extracted from South America by Spain and Portugal. The money did not stay in Spain but spilled over into the rest of Western Europe through trade and sometimes piracy on the high seas. Europe's stock of precious metals, which in 1492 was estimated at 35 million pounds sterling, went up to 87 million pounds sterling by 1599.[1]

Prices rose rapidly. Across Western Europe between 1492 and 1589, they rose by between 400 percent and 700 percent depending on the particular country you look at. Wages rose faster than prices. Soon Spanish traders encountered difficulties in selling their goods abroad but found they could import from anywhere in the world. (This was later to be called the Dutch Disease where a national currency appreciates so much that exports are expensive for your customers abroad but imports from abroad are cheap for your citizens.) The gold that flowed out of Spain and into France, England and Holland to purchase goods for the Spaniards caused a boom in those countries and with it higher employment and higher prices. But Europe was not where the money rested; it flowed out abroad. In trade with India and Southeast Asia and the Middle East, Europe bought the silks and spices and other luxury goods but had to pay with gold because Europe had no commodities which the Easterners wanted. People felt bewildered. They wondered if the stability of their previous lives was lost. What was constant and what had changed? Were there stable "values" underneath the fast-changing prices? Was money, with its swift arrival and even quicker departure, like women who seduced by their charms and then vanished?

The Iberian loot of South America caused a "century of inflation" between the mid-sixteenth and mid-seventeenth centuries in Western Europe. Economics was no longer a study of household management as originally conceived by the Greeks, who coined the term. It now had to deal with the fortunes of nations and people, of movements of precious metals and the influence they had on prices and wages and incomes at home and abroad. How did money determine prices, the level of exports and imports, wages and employment?

The importance of gold and silver within the country as an indicator of wealth was recognized. Public policy was redirected to exporting goods to obtain gold but economizing on imports to prevent gold from being lost. Gold and silver equaled wealth. Wars and territorial conquests were seen as an alternative but expensive means of acquiring gold, as the Spaniards had proved. But the questions raised by the influx of treasures became increasingly urgent. Was gold an accurate representation of the wealth of a country, and why did the influx of gold and silver cause prices to rise? The answers came from two intellectual titans of the time.

John Locke (1632–1704) was born in a Puritan family and grew up while England was going through the Civil War. It was a conflict rooted in differences of religious beliefs between Catholics and Protestants but perpetuated by disagreement on how the kingdom should be governed. Locke's most celebrated book was written in this spirit and led him to be exiled to Holland. *Two Treatises on Government* questioned the theory of the divine right of kings and affirmed the rights of subjects to remove their king if his conduct did not meet with their approval. When the English aristocracy rose against James II and invited

William of Orange (from Holland) and his wife, Mary, to take over the throne of England, Locke's influence was very much behind the move. Locke's argument about the right of subjects to revolt was invoked a century later by the American colonies when they rose in revolt against the British.

Once back in England with the new king and queen, Locke's power grew. He organized the Board of Trade to further foreign trade and became its Commissioner from 1695 to 1700. In those days, usury laws prevailed and Parliament would set the rate of interest. Parliament proposed to lower the rate from 6 percent to 4 percent. Locke argued that the interest rate being the price at which money was hired, it would be regulated by the demand for and the supply of money. All prices were determined by demand and supply and could not be dictated by the state. Locke was thus a pioneer in defining equilibrium (a word which he used) as being determined "naturally" by individual activity in the market.

He also pioneered a theory of inflation. He argued that money had value because it enabled people to buy goods and services. Its value would be inversely related to its quantity in circulation. The idea that blood circulated through the human body had recently been proved by William Harvey, who, like Locke, was a doctor. The notion that money also circulates was a natural extension. The more money there was in circulation the less its value would be. In other words too much money relative to goods available would cause inflation. How and why this happened would take centuries to figure out but for many ordinary people the idea that too much money relative to goods resulted in rising prices – inflation – became the only bit of economics they intuitively understood.

Locke's arguments were refined by David Hume (1711–76). Hume was a multifaceted genius. He was a philosopher, a historian and an economist. Religion had been a big issue in the seventeenth century. Now skepticism about the beliefs of earlier ages was spreading. Hume was a rationalist. His book *A Treatise on Human Nature*, written when he was 26, is acclaimed as a classic work. He traveled extensively to the continent, where he befriended Jean-Jacques Rousseau among others. He was the first major philosopher who also wrote extensively on economic issues of trade, money and exchange. Hume developed Locke's argument further. He showed that the influx of precious metals was a double-edged sword which had the initial effect of increasing economic activity by creating jobs, encouraging manufactures and increasing trade. But eventually, if money kept flooding in from outside (as was the case with Spain in the previous two centuries), there would be limits to how far economic activity could expand in the short term, and this constraint would result in inflation. As to the question of what constituted wealth, the answer was to come from a fellow Scotsman and friend – Adam Smith.

Determining the Wealth of Nations

Adam Smith, a lifelong bachelor who lived with his mother and sister all his adult life, was a friend of David Hume. Smith was elected a Professor of Moral Philosophy at Glasgow, and later gave up the post to become a tutor to the Duke of Buccleuch, which allowed him to travel all over Europe meeting the famous philosophers of his day. Smith revolutionized the way we conduct our lives and governments their policies. In the eighteenth century, kings still sought to increase their wealth through invasion and plunder – Britain was even then in the middle of its long century of war with France, which lasted, on and off, from 1695 to 1815. In his celebrated book *An Inquiry into the Nature and Causes of the Wealth of Nations*, published in 1776, Adam Smith pointed out that it was the productivity of its workers which was the key to the prosperity of a nation and not the treasures of gold and silver it had accumulated. The productivity of the workers could be enhanced with tools and machines. The capital – the money to buy the tools and machinery as well as to pay the wages – was accumulated out of the profits that the providers of capital made by employing the workers. Workers who were employed by capital made goods with a value above what they were paid, that is, their output generated a profit above their wage. They were *productive* workers. Workers employed as servants by their master for daily help generated no surplus above their wage and hence were *unproductive* workers. Employing productive workers was an investment, while hiring workers as domestic servants was consumption. A nation had to divert its wealth from employing unproductive workers to employing productive ones. That was the way of increasing its wealth. The most productive workers were those who specialized in an activity – who were part of a division of labor.

When shopping for groceries, we rarely contemplate how the goods that we are purchasing were produced. But if we were to take a loaf of bread, for example, its arrival at the store would have involved the cooperation of the farmer, the miller, the baker and the truck driver. Each of the links in this chain has its own connections, with the farmer, for example, relying on the suppliers of water, fertilizers, equipment, labor and veterinary assistance, to name just a few. This Smith termed the division of labor, whereby people specialize within a factory and across industries to be more productive. All this cooperation is done not so much by diktat from above or due to the kindness of the many people who brought the bread to you; it is because they all stand to make a living out of supplying the bread to you.

Of course, in the olden days there were self-sufficient house-holds and even self-sufficient villages which conducted only limited trade with the outside world. But as the scope of the market expanded – thanks to roads and ease of transport – the division of labor became more extensive and now no household or village or even nation remains self-sufficient. This is a mark of prosperity despite the persistence of the appeal of the self-sufficiency model for nationalists.

The complex voluntary cooperation which exists beneath the surface of our daily economic life was called the *invisible hand* by Adam Smith. It is the interdependence of people far-flung and unknown to each other which is the most difficult thing to grasp about economics. It is wondrous that the myriad separate decisions made by millions of individuals about what to buy and what to sell, what to produce, which job to take and where to study ultimately hang together to ensure that when you go to the shops there are things to buy that you want, that there are jobs to go to for most of us and that the same will be the case tomorrow. It is as if, as Adam Smith said, an invisible hand is guiding us.

The invisible hand is not always benevolent. It may also work adversely. Why else would the bankruptcy of a New York firm, Lehman's, cause unemployment in Lancashire? Why would we debate the prospect of the eurozone or worry about Chinese growth causing petrol prices to rise? The complex interconnectedness threaded together by myriad independent decisions is central to an understanding of why economics is such a difficult and uncertain subject.

Each individual deciding to buy or postpone a purchase, or to take up a job or wait for a better one, acts on their own impulses and it is hoped uses their powers of reasoning as well. They are unpredictable individually. But collectively the decisions form a pattern. Think of what might happen if physical objects had a mind of their own and acted of their own volition. The apple that fell on Newton's head inspired the theory of gravity. But if an apple had its own volition, it might well have decided not to come down but to go back up to its perch. The subject matter of economics consists of individuals with volition. unlike the subjects of natural science. The economist's hope is that while individual agents may have their own reasons for behaving any way they like, as a group their behavior will show some regularity and predictability. Devices such as the invisible hand are ways of coping with this complexity so that we can grasp its working.

Adam Smith's other powerful idea was that in order to generate and guarantee prosperity, there should be minimal restrictions on people's choices. Governments should stick to providing law and order, guarantee secure property rights, create fair and broad-based taxes, spend prudently on matters such as education and infrastructure, and keep the budget in balance. Allowing people "to do their own thing," as we would put it today, would maximize prosperity. He called this the System of Natural Liberty.

In those days, the economy was riddled with monopolies granted by Royal Charter to companies such as the East India Company, which controlled all Eastern trade; rules of guilds as to who could enter a profession; and tolls and taxes on movement of goods across the country. Governments were interfering in every occupation and every kind of business, while being corrupt and inefficient at the same time. Much of the revenue received was spent on war, and when the revenue could not be collected the governments borrowed from the merchants and goldsmiths, or worse, clipped their coins to fool the people. In contemporary France, the tolls on movement of food grains were such that often famine in one part could not be relieved by bringing food from other parts. It was in response to one such incident that a group of businessmen in France told the King's Finance Minister, Colbert, "Laissez-nous passez; laissez-nous faire" [Let us pass; let us do things ourselves]. Adam Smith never used the expression laissez-faire but the idea of letting the economy be free of odious restrictions on the movement of goods and people caught on. Indeed, when the French Revolution broke out, many blamed it on the radical ideas of Adam Smith!

In his earlier book *The Theory of Moral Sentiments* (1759), Adam Smith had expressed a distrust of someone trying to regulate a society from above. "The man of system," he wrote,

> seems to imagine that he can arrange the different members of a great society with as much ease as the hand that arranges the different pieces on a chess-board; he does not consider that the different pieces upon a chess-board have no other principle of motion besides that which the hand impresses upon them; but that, in the great chess-board of human society, every single piece has a principle of motion of its own. Altogether different from that which the legislator might choose to impress upon it.[2]

The "Principle of Motion"

Adam Smith and his Scottish contemporaries were part of the Scottish Enlightenment. They founded what we now consider to be the social sciences. They were deeply impressed by Isaac

Newton's achievement in astronomy, delineating the principles upon which the planets moved in a systematic way unaided by any explicit agency. It was said that Newton had discovered God's system of how the heavens worked. Smith and his fellow Scotsmen wanted to discover the principles of social astronomy, as it were: what made societies function and evolve, grow or decay. Newton had based his work on the unifying principle of gravity. Was there such a unifying principle in human societies? Smith found the principle in self-interest. Not selfishness but self-interest. He was well aware of the role of benevolence and sympathy in social life, which he had discussed in *The Theory of Moral Sentiments*. There were restraints on the pursuit of self-interest by individuals in the laws of the land as well as social conventions. But the dynamic energy unleashed by millions of people pursuing self-interest was the key to the wealth of nations.

Adam Smith was a Deist, that is, someone who did not believe in the Revelation or the Virgin Birth but was religious. The fashionable doctrine in those days was of God as a Clockmaker. God did not intervene in the mundane affairs of the people on earth. He set the universe in motion as if it were a highly sprung and delicate clock which then worked away on its own as the pendulum swung back and forth. This was a non-interfering God who set the rules of the game and then let people play it according to their wishes and ability. The invisible hand was a similar idea of a sort of secular rather than divine mechanism to coordinate the myriad activities of separate individuals, buying and selling, working and saving, investing and exporting.

But no one is actually in charge; we all are on our separate ways. The idea of society as a self-organizing entity that Smith and the Scottish Enlightenment gifted to posterity comes from such notions about how the world works. Isaac Newton's theory about the movements of planets also fitted in with this idea. The universe was obeying the laws of motion (implicitly set by God long ago and discovered by Newton) and no one was driving the planets on a daily basis.

Once it was understood that the economy was a complex web of mutually interdependent relations, with each person pursuing their own interest and yet arriving at a good outcome, it was easy to see the international system as just an extension of this idea. Exports should be encouraged freely and so should imports. Countries that insisted on exporting goods but conserving the gold earned in return (a policy known as mercantilism) were short-sighted. A country's wealth would be determined by obtaining the largest amount of goods and services as cheaply as possible. Nowadays, it is commonplace to import a variety of products from abroad, from agricultural produce to technological goods, because it is cheaper than making these products at home. Other countries face the same problem and hence they import our goods into their country. But it was a novel idea in Smith's time. Producing goods cheaply is dependent on the productivity of workers, assisted by machinery in industrial production and by fertile land in agriculture. As long as people are free to set up industries, employ workers and make profits, the country will have an abundant supply of cheap goods and services. Workers get wages, capitalists get profits and landlords get rent, since in agriculture land is an essential input. If the capital is borrowed from a bank or some other creditor, interest has to be paid on that. The sum of wages, profits, rent and interest is income.

Today, interest is an integral part of the financial system. When we borrow money from a financial institution it is based on the understanding that we will have to pay the original sum plus an additional amount determined by the rate of interest added. But interest was not a simple matter back then. There was the biblical injunction against usury. The Old Testament forbade Jews from charging interest on loans to their fellow Jews (though not on those to Gentiles). The Sermon on the Mount was even more prohibitive. Aristotle had reasoned that money was barren and could not, and indeed should not, bear fruit. Interest charged on money was thus suspect. But, of course, borrowing and lending was rife. Kings were always in need of money to fight wars, as their subjects did not like paying taxes for the wars. Lombards, who were some of the earliest bankers in modern Europe, called themselves money changers – foreign exchange dealers as we would call them. But they also loaned to kings. Jews were also active in the loan market as long as the borrower was not one of their fellow Jews, which kings seldom were. Lending to kings was a risky business because they often refused to pay the loan back and used force if the lender complained. Wise kings, however, knew they might need to borrow again and so they paid up. Bankers insisted on freedom for their occupations or the "freedom of the city" where they worked in order to insure against the king's predations.

The ban on usury meant that the law often regulated the amount of interest that could be charged on loans. But money could generate income in many ways, not just by pure usury. Money advanced for productive purposes generates yield which is similar to interest but need not be usury. Fathers of the Church had to advise members of their flock, who often had awkward questions. Could a widow live off the rent of a property her husband had left her or was it usury and hence sinful? What was legitimate income from investment – profits – and what was usury, interest? The separation of interest on idle money from profits made from investing the money in some enterprise was thought through by the medieval Scholastics as they perused their Bibles and studied commentaries. The early revolution in banking which began in Italy threw up many such questions for the religious authorities to deal with. Renaissance was followed by Reformation and a veritable transformation in the attitude toward trade and accumulation. The modern world wanted to be free as far as it could from such old-fashioned restrictions. Smith caught the spirit of the times

Adam Smith also wrote on the perennial problem of inflation. He proposed a startling new way of viewing price volatility, a problem that had been plaguing the European economies for the past couple of centuries. Given that the intrinsic *value* of the commodity had not changed – it was the same commodity but with a different price – one had to distinguish between the money price of a commodity and its value. An increase in the money price of output was illusory if the higher price was due to inflation. He argued that the value of a commodity should be measured by the amount of productive labor needed to produce it. That did not mean that lazy workers who took twice as long as active workers produced goods of higher value. Competition between producers ensured that goods were produced most efficiently with minimal labor time. But the less time each unit required, the larger the basket of commodities produced and that basket was the income of the country. The crucial thing was to understand what determined the value of one good relative to another: cloth and shoes, for example. This could be understood without looking at their prices but by comparing how much labor time it took to manufacture one relative to another. For an economy where the machines were still more like tools than elaborate assembly lines, labor was the most important input. The capital which assisted the worker was comprised of easily made and replaceable tools. The machine's contribution to the good also had to be measured in labor time. This was to cause problems later on when machinery became elaborate. But for the time when Smith was writing, it was possible to argue that values were the centers of gravity to which prices converged once the effects of money had been neutralized. Values were stable; prices volatile.

Since Adam Smith was a Professor of Moral Philosophy, the *Wealth of Nations* was written in the style of a philosopher with a broad sweep of history and knowledge of almost the entire world and its activities. It was a bestseller. His ideas were forceful – that there was a coordinating mechanism which worked without anyone driving it, that the best results were obtained by leaving people alone to follow their pursuits, and that the wealth of a country lay in the abundance of the goods and services that its people could afford to consume thanks to the productivity of its workers and the enterprise of the employers – and his advice was adopted by the government of the day. William Pitt the Younger, then Prime Minister, invited him to Downing Street and insisted that out of respect for Smith, the Cabinet stood while Smith sat and gave them advice. Smith established the usefulness of political economy, as the subject came to be called; it was a combination of philosophy, history, economic theory and some practical economic policy advice.

The Certainties of David Ricardo

The years which followed Adam Smith's death in 1790 were turbulent for Europe. Britain had already lost its colonies in North America. The Rebels had issued a Declaration of Independence in the same year the *Wealth of Nations* was published and defeated the mother country in a series of decisive battles. They had established the first republic in many centuries in 1789, the same year the French Revolution broke out. In 1793 King Louis XVI of France was beheaded and a French Republic was established. Britain went to war with France to restore the Old Monarchy in a coalition with other European kingdoms and after 22 years defeated the French at Waterloo in 1815. These years saw wide-spread political as well as economic turbulence. Inspired by the French Revolution and Adam Smith's radical ideas, people imagined that the society they lived in could be much better. The Old Order of kings and the aristocrats could be, and indeed should be, overthrown. In 1794, William Godwin wrote *An Enquiry Concerning Political Justice and Its Influence on General Virtue and Happiness*. This took Smith's idea of the burden of regulations to its extreme and argued that Political Justice would only be established when rational people removed all political institutions and shunned all sentimental attachments. This was a utopia of human beings who were "perfectible," to use a phrase Rousseau had made fashionable. Wordsworth, Coleridge, Hazlitt and Shelley were among the many enthusiastic and impressionable young men who were swept away by the power of Godwin's arguments. Champions of the French Revolution identified with Godwin, though he admired Edmund Burke, a virulent enemy of the Revolution.

But there was economic turbulence as well. Inflation, the old specter of a century ago, had raised its head again. To combat inflation in the earlier century, the pound sterling had been based on its value in terms of gold, £3 17s 10½d per ounce, a price fixed by Sir Isaac Newton when he was Master of the Mint. (This price held until 1933.) Citizens could take gold to be coined at the Mint and offer their coins to get gold if they wanted. The pound was convertible into gold. Banknotes issued by the Bank of England were also convertible into gold – the £20 note still bears the legend "I promise to pay the bearer on demand the sum of twenty pounds."

Today it means two notes of £10 or four of £5. In those days it meant gold coin equivalent. Under the Gold Standard, if too much money was issued which resulted in price hikes in goods, the demand for imports increased and so gold left the country to pay for imports. This in turn led to a shrinkage of the money supply and prices fell as a consequence. That was how the Gold Standard forced an automatic adjustment, or at least that was the theory.

Set up a century earlier by William Paterson as a private entity with shareholders, the Bank of England's principal function was to secure funds for the king. Paterson had long held the view that the nation's finances were in disarray, not least because of its continued involvement in wars. It also had no real system of money and credit. Following the Battle of Beachy Head in 1690, where the British Navy was defeated, William III required funds to rebuild. In return for this help, the Bank was given a monopoly of issuing notes, which became widely used in place of coins. The Bank's issue of notes was regulated by the movement of the gold price. The notes were convertible into gold at any time they were presented to the Bank. The Bank of England would have to pay out gold if the holders of notes thought gold attracted a higher price abroad than in England. The Bank would then have to raise its interest rate to attract gold back. Similarly, if the exports were buoyant and too much gold came in, the interest rate would be cut.

In 1797 the Bank of England had to suspend the link. The Anglo-French War was draining too much gold abroad from the coffers of the Bank. Thus the Bank's reserves of gold were depleted and it was unable to convert notes into gold at the rate previously possible. If people had come to the Bank to convert their notes into gold, the bank would have had to declare bankruptcy. To resolve this situation, paper currency was introduced which was non-convertible into gold. Under the Gold Standard, the amount of money issued was regulated by the amount of gold available in the Bank of England's coffers. With paper currency, there was no such guidance. Inflation soon followed. War helped to mitigate some of the effects by expanding economic activity, but inflation was ever present. The value of the paper pound fell in terms of the Dutch florin on the Amsterdam Stock Exchange.

Had the Bank Issued Excess Currency?

It fell to David Ricardo to open the debate on the causes of the depreciation of the pound. In a pamphlet called "On the High Price of Bullion," the first that he wrote, he showed that the best way to measure how much excess paper currency the Bank of England had issued would be to work out the percentage depreciation of the pound on the foreign exchange from the time when the link with gold was broken. Ricardo's pamphlet created controversy and Parliament appointed a committee to examine the problem. The report of the Parliamentary committee, called the Bullion Report, confirmed Ricardo's calculation. After all, they were just confirming the basic truth of John Locke's theory on inflation but expanded to include an international context.

David Ricardo (1772–1823) was a most unusual man. If Adam Smith was a reclusive philosopher, Ricardo was a busy man of affairs – stockbroker, landowner and, in his last years, Member of Parliament. He had shown no interest in matters of philosophical speculation. From his activities in the stock market and as an agent who sold government debt – a loan-contractor, as the role was called – he made a vast fortune which made him a landowner in his later years. He had a house in Grosvenor Square (later the site of the US Embassy) and a country estate in Gatcombe Park (later the place lived in by the Princess Royal, Princess Anne).

Ricardo was born into a Jewish family which had originally been Spanish-Portuguese but had been driven out by the persecution of Jews during the Inquisition, and his ancestors had settled in Holland and carried on the trade of stockbrokers. His father, Abraham Israel Ricardo, was a member of the Amsterdam Stock Exchange where he dealt in government debt and options. He later moved to England, where David Ricardo was born. Ricardo had no university education, having been inducted into his father's business at 14. At the age of 21, he fell in love with a Quaker woman and renounced Judaism to become a Christian. While visiting his convalescing wife in Bath one day, he happened to come across Adam Smith's *Wealth of Nations* in the local library, and immediately thought that he could make many of its propositions logically much tighter.

Ricardo ended up creating economics as we recognize it today. Smith's speculations on the invisible hand became in Ricardo's hands a theory of the markets in which equilibrium between demand and supply was guaranteed as long as competition prevailed. Indeed markets could never be out of equilibrium unless governments imposed artificial restraints on economic activity. What Smith expressed with a penumbra of qualifications, Ricardo asserted as a law. Political economy was no longer a branch of moral philosophy; in Ricardo's hands it became a science.

Much more important to our purpose was a debate between Ricardo and his friend Thomas Robert Malthus about whether there could be a temporary "glut"; could there be a situation in which more would be supplied than there was a demand for? More being demanded than was supplied caused inflation, but this was the other side of the coin. Malthus pointed out that the cessation of the Anglo-French War after 1815 had led to a retrenchment in government expenditure. This reduction in government expenditure in turn meant that many private businesses shut down, with many workers becoming unemployed. Ricardo again and again irrefutably "proved" by his superior and unrelenting logic that supply and demand were two sides of the same coin. "Supply created its own demand." All capital which is being used in some industry or another will command a profit. Labor will be employed in making things as long as it is productive enough to justify the wages paid to it. If a laborer is unemployed, it could only be a result of insisting on too high a wage. This was Say's Law, named after the French economist Jean-Baptiste Say. A market economy is always in equilibrium. There can be no glut, no depression by definition. Echoes of Ricardo still reverberate in modern academies.

It may puzzle people why economists should be fascinated by such an unrealistic theory. Keynes, who was to attempt the most serious challenge to Ricardo's theory, wrote eloquently about this:

> For since Malthus was unable to explain clearly (apart from an appeal to the facts of common observation) how and why effective demand could be deficient or excessive, he failed to furnish an alternative construction; and Ricardo conquered England as completely as the Holy Inquisition conquered Spain. Not only was his theory accepted by the city, by statesmen and by the academic world. But controversy ceased; the other point of view completely disappeared; it ceased to be discussed . . .
>
> The completeness of the Ricardian victory is something of a curiosity and a mystery. That it reached conclusions quite different from what the ordinary uninstructed persons would expect added, I suppose, to its intellectual prestige. That its teaching translated into practice, was austere and often unpalatable, lent it virtue. That it was adapted to carry a vast and consistent logical superstructure, gave it beauty.[3]

The doctrine for which Ricardo is perhaps best known concerns how countries should conduct trade and why. Of course, a country should import goods that are cheaper to import from abroad than to make at home and export those it could make cheaper than other countries. But Ricardo argued that out of two commodities, with cloth and wine as his examples, even if England could make both wine and cloth at a lower cost – measured in terms of labor time – than say Portugal, it should concentrate on whichever was the less costly of the two and import the other. Each country had to look at the *comparative advantage* it had, since that would guarantee better use of its resources. It is a proposition which defies common sense and yet he argued it logically and convinced generations of economists, and indeed many politicians (though not all), that countries should follow the logic of comparative advantage. Politicians instinctively prefer protectionism, which would advise both countries to produce both goods and put barriers on trade between them. Smith had argued for free trade but Ricardo made it into a powerful doctrine. It has remained to this day a bedrock of international economic relationships.

Ricardo also ascertained an iron law of wages. Wages would not rise above subsistence level in the long run since any rise would be nullified by a rise in population, as his friend Malthus had demonstrated in the Law of Population. Malthus had shown that food to sustain the population only increased in an arithmetical progression, 1, 2, 3, 4. But population increased in a geometric progression, 1, 2, 4, 8, 16. The only reason why this had not already happened was that vice (loose morals, etc.) and misery (poverty, starvation) acted as checks on the growth of population. The Law was inexorable. Remove misery and vice and you will be overwhelmed by the growth of population. The inexorable logic of the Law of Population argued against the feasibility of a Rational Utopia and so denied Godwin's Utopian vision.

Ricardo argued that a growing population would result in increased competition for jobs. With more workers competing for jobs, there would be downward pressure on wages. However, Combinations, or trade unions as they are now called, restricted the free movement of labor and hence were harmful. They raised the wages of their members, but reduced the prospect of employment for the generality of workers. He also established as a universal truth of economics that the rate of profit would be the same in all parts of the economy as long as there were no restrictions on the movement of money capital between activities.

His most radical doctrine was to show that rent – the economic return that land should accrue to landlords when used in production – was an unearned income; the price of corn was set by the cost of producing corn on the least fertile land under the plough. All "superior" lands earned a rent since the cost of cultivation was much lower on superior lands compared to the marginal, least fertile land. Rent was just a surplus based on the cost of obtaining corn from the marginal land. As the population grew or prosperity increased, the demand for food would rise and more and more marginal land would need to be cultivated. Rent on superior land would increase with no effort on the part of the landlord. He asserted this despite being a landlord himself.

Ricardo reinterpreted Smith's assertion that the values of various commodities could be established without any reference to money and firmly established it within modern economics in terms of money as a scaling variable. The "relative" value (value in exchange) of one good in terms of another, of shoes in terms of cloth, was determined by the amount of labor embodied in each – the minimum amount of time it took to produce each product efficiently with the technology available The effect of money (capital) would be reflected in labor time, and profit rates would be the same across all activities. If it takes two hours to make a pair of shoes and ten hours to make a table, the table will exchange for five pairs of shoes. But if there was a better division of labor in the carpentry shop, the table might be made in four hours. Then the table would exchange for only two pairs of shoes.

This simplification was to cause many problems for Ricardo and many subsequent theorists. How machinery modified the value of a commodity measured in labor time was a complex issue which defeated even Ricardo. Machines were made by labor and other machines. Even if you could measure the cost of producing the machines in terms of the amount of time it took laborers to build them, what of the money invested in making the machine in the meantime? Should the interest charged on that money enter into the value of the commodity? If machines replaced manual labor, how would that alter the value of a commodity measured in labor time? This problem of capital – machinery or durable goods in general – was to haunt economics over the years.

The amount of money available determined the money price level, or the nominal level, as economists now call it. In the classical theory as expounded by Ricardo, it has no effect on the real workings of the economy except to move all the prices up and down together. People in daily life notice money prices, not values or relative prices. This is because money is a veil which hides the real workings of the economy.

The role of money as a scaling variable is still a basic argument in modern economics, especially in what I have called mainstream modern macroeconomics. Money is separate from the real economy and is useful to establish the rate of inflation in the economy.

Modern economists use a lot of algebra and equations and numbers to demonstrate this but Ricardo was the person who, without the use of any mathematics, proved these propositions by logical deduction. Thus for Ricardo and later economic theorists, the economy can be perpetually in equilibrium as long as no outside restraints are imposed. The economy achieves equilibrium of its own volition and more or less instantaneously. It is a puzzle that a practical man of business proved something which is so theoretical and, many would say, in contradiction to the facts of life. Yet his abstractions determined forever the content of economics and the style of economists.

A Dismal Science?

Ricardo had argued that the iron law of wages would not hold up if there were technological innovations. Even today, it is hard to imagine the types of technological innovations that may be invented in the future and how they will impact our working lives. And so the Ricardians became known for their iron law of wages and a generally pessimistic view of the world. Ricardo had feared that as time passed, the population grew and the economy developed, profitable opportunities would dry up. With a growing population, rent would increase since land was fixed in supply and agricultural techniques were given. Out of the total revenue, with wages fixed by an iron law and rent rising, the burden would fall on profits, which would fall. Thus, as a consequence of progress, the rate of profit would fall. As profits fell and investment dried up the economy would reach a stationary state. This would be a high-income, zero-growth economy. There was not much anyone could do about it except keep the budget balanced and prices low.

Ricardo gave subsequent generations of economists the confidence that economic analysis could be applied to any given situation. Successive generations of economists took up the challenge. In the mid-nineteenth century in Britain there was controversy about the abolition of slavery in the Caribbean islands. Thomas Carlyle was among the many conservative writers who predicted that this would have negative economic consequences when there would be no one to harvest the sugar cane and other crops. John Stuart Mill responded by saying that when slavery was abolished, the market would find substitute forms of labor. This would be similar to slavery but with free people. This is indeed what happened; indentured labor was brought in from India and elsewhere to fill the gap. Carlyle denounced economics as a dismal science for this reason. But Mill was right to support the abolition of slavery and predict that market forces would find substitute labor. It was the universal development of the markets for commodities, labor and capital which inspired the next stage of development in economic theory.

Mathematics of the Markets

The next step in the development of economics was the attempt to put Ricardo's theory of equilibrium into mathematics. That was the contribution of the Frenchman Léon Walras (1834–1910). Léon Walras thought of himself as a socialist despite having been a stockbroker journalist and manager of a cooperative bank in his youth. He tried to train himself to become an engineer but found that not to his liking. He wrote a novel and worked in the railways for a while. Walras's father, Antoine Auguste Walras, had tried to develop a theory of value on the basis of the scarcity of a commodity relative to the demand for it. Walras Senior was familiar with mathematical methods and directed his son to other French works, such as that by Antoine Augustin Cournot, who had used mathematics to address economic issues. As his interest in economics developed, Léon Walras found it difficult to secure a university position in France. All the major professorships were taken and if a vacancy arose it went to one of the students of the Professor. His work, however, soon attracted the attention of the University of Lausanne in Switzerland, where he was later to became a professor of economics.

Walras's lasting contribution to economics was to represent the theories of Smith and Ricardo in an elegant mathematical form. Before he could do this, he had to convince the economic profession to abandon the labor theory of value, which Smith, Ricardo and others had advanced. Walras was supported by two notable economists, the English W. Stanley Jevons (1835–88) and the Austrian Carl Menger (1840–1921). The value of a good, they argued, was no longer determined by the amount of labor time contained. It was the result of its scarcity, which stemmed from consumers' preferences for the good based on the utility – satisfaction – gained from its consumption and also the resources required to produce it. The consumer would compare the utility of a good and its price with the utility and price of other goods that she could also consume. This process would result in the demand for the various goods. The producer would compare the returns she could get from producing an alternative good – the opportunity cost of doing what she did. From these considerations would come the supply of goods. There was to be no distinction between value and price. Price as determined by the market was value and value was measured by price.

Walras formulated the idea that the demand for each good was a function of its own price and the prices of all other goods against which it could be compared. Similarly for supply. Labor demand and supply could tell us how many people would be employed, for example, and thereby what their wage would be and therefore the total wage bill. If more workers were available than were demanded at a certain wage rate, the wage would fall until demand and supply were equal. Similarly if more workers were demanded than were available, wages would rise until demand and supply were in equilibrium. For hundreds of such goods and services their demand and supply would equilibrate simultaneously at a specific price. Here was the invisible hand of Adam Smith formulated mathematically as an instant solution which showed how the prices of all the goods and services were formed. One device to bring them into equilibrium would be to imagine that there was an auctioneer, as was the case on the Paris Bourse with which Walras was familiar. The auctioneer would announce a price of a share and then would invite bids and offers. He would tweak the price up and down till the bids matched the offers. Walras called the adjustment of price up and down *tatonnement*.

Money did not play a role in this formulation. It was breathtakingly elegant, simple and highly unrealistic. It was its elegance alongside its simplicity which appealed to economists. Ricardo's endorsements of Say's Law of the markets was now given a mathematical garb, thus making it even more forceful and convincing than a merely verbal formulation. Walras had now given economics a *theory of general equilibrium*.

In a world which is always in equilibrium, there can be no crises, no cycles. Even more elegant was the formulation that if competition prevailed, profits would be driven to zero by capitalists undercutting each other. Profits as a category disappeared from economics. Walras proved to be even more logically pure than Ricardo and even more unrealistic. Walras's formulations have allowed modern economists to display their mathematical ingenuity in refining and extending his ideas.

Gerard Debreu, a Frenchman who settled in the United States and taught at Berkeley, the University of California, was awarded the Nobel Prize in Economics in 1983 for his research which proved Walras's theory with much more up-to-date and rigorous mathematical tools. When journalists asked him for his views on the problem of inflation, which was then worrying everyone, he said frankly that the kind of economics he did, did not enable him to pronounce on such practical questions!

Chapter Two

CYCLES FOR THE CURIOUS

Where Do Cycles Come From?

One generation after Ricardo and Malthus had debated the crisis, the world had changed beyond recognition. The Gold Standard had been abandoned in 1797 but in 1821, after the end of the war, orthodox opinion insisted on returning to it. Severe hardships followed as debts incurred in inflationary times, when real interest rates were low, had to be paid back. Prices had since fallen and interest rates risen. The National Debt that had been incurred during the war also had to be paid back. It placed a heavy burden on the Exchequer, leaving little money for amelioration of the misery of the people. There was agrarian unrest across England, with farmers burning hayracks and causing extensive damage. In 1825 there was a another crisis. This was not just a matter of the retrenchment of expenditure after the end of the war, as had happened in 1816. This time was different. It was the first run on the banks and the first collapse of companies as a consequence. It was the first time in living memory that workers had become unemployed due to reasons beyond even their employers' control. After this episode, crises began to recur with some regularity in England. A crisis would interrupt a period of normalcy or even prosperity. But once the crisis had occurred, things reversed and distress spread. Shops and factories shut down and workers were out of work. Eventually there was a recovery until the next crisis.

The nature of the economy had changed from being a predominantly agrarian and rural economy with small handicraft workshops to an industrial economy. The Industrial Revolution had proceeded apace and country after country had witnessed the destruction of its traditional crafts and the installation of factories. Spinning had been revolutionized in the previous century. The use of steam power had also radically transformed mining, transport and trade. Cotton was being imported from around the world, especially from the American South where slave labor guaranteed cheap supplies. The cloth made from cheap yarn replaced the cottage workshops across the world, beginning in England itself. People were leaving their villages and flocking into factories in cities. Oliver Goldsmith was already lamenting *The Deserted Village* in his poem of 1770.

Business was also much more dependent on credit than was the case in an agrarian economy. Large investments were required and the people who made these investments – the capitalists – were taking risks, although with the expectation of high returns. The coordinating mechanism of the invisible hand was perhaps occasionally failing to direct matters to a beneficent end.

Ricardian theory denied such a possibility. There could be only be gluts and unemployment if workers were demanding too high wages. But the misery was recurring and palpable. People sought an answer to their problems. Early debates on the causes of crises blamed them on monetary factors. When the convertibility of bank notes had been suspended in 1797 it was because of a run on the Bank of England. As Henry Thornton, an astute banker, wrote at that time:

> The causes which lead to a variation in the rapidity of circulation of bank notes may be several . . . a high state of confidence contributes to make men provide less amply against contingencies . . . When on the contrary, a season of distrust arises, prudence suggests that the loss of interest arising from a detention of notes for a few additional days should not be disregarded.[1]

This marks the importance of the rise and fall of confidence as a force in a modern monetary economy. Money and its pathology became subjects of debate from here on.

The money problem was not just an English concern. Across the Atlantic the fledgling Republic was also mired in controversies about money and banks. The American Revolution had been financed with paper money and IOUs issued by the revolutionary army. After independence, when the Republic was founded,

Alexander Hamilton, the first Secretary of the Treasury, established the Bank of the United States. He took over the debts issued by the colonies which had declared independence from Britain and consolidated the public finances. This, however, also meant severe deflation and again it was the farmers who had incurred debts in good times when money was plentiful who paid the price of the collapse in prices. Banks and banking became a perennial subject of political debate in America from then on. The agrarian populists following Thomas Jefferson were suspicious of the banks and opposed to Hamilton's reforms. The controversy again erupted when Andrew Jackson, elected President in 1828, vetoed the renewal of the Charter of the Second Bank of the United States. On both sides of the Atlantic farmers favored easy money, while financiers and business people liked balanced budgets and sound money.

In Great Britain, when the crisis of 1825 occurred, people harked back to the experience during the years of the paper currency when the pound was suspended from the Gold Standard. These had been years of war and high levels of employment. There was inflation but also a lot of prosperity. "Money cranks" – named because they defied the Ricardian orthodoxy – began arguing that it was the restriction of money and credit imposed by the Gold Standard which was causing crises. If currency was plentiful and the pound could be depreciated (as had been the case during the Anglo-French wars) all would be well. Low prices were at the center of the problem and some means had to be found to generate inflation. In Birmingham, then a center of many small and middle-size enterprises, Thomas Attwood and his brother Mathias became known as monetary agitators arguing for reform. As Thomas said in evidence to the Committee on the Bank of England Charter in 1832:

> As a general principle, I think, unquestionably, that so long as any number of industrious honest workmen in the Kingdom are out of employment, supposing such deficiency of employment not to be local but general, I should think it the duty, and certainly the interest, of Government, to continue the depreciation of the currency until full employment is obtained and general prosperity.[2]

This line of argument – a policy of inflation to cure unemployment – has remained in fashion since the days of Thomas Attwood, although its theoretical garb has improved. But there were other economists who sought the reasons for the shock and the recurrence – almost cyclical – of the pattern of prosperity and slumps in non-monetary or real factors. Was it something in the nature of the industrial economy and the capitalist's willingness to venture his investments in the hope of profit which could be at the root of the recurrence of prosperity and misery?

A Revolution in Thinking

Fifty years after the mechanization of spinning, weaving was also transformed into a mechanical activity. Handloom weavers everywhere were thrown out of work. Among them were the weavers of Silesia on the border of Germany and Poland. A young philosopher who had been blackballed from academic jobs had taken up journalism as a profession. He stumbled across the distress of the Silesian weavers. That took him to reading political economy, as economics was still called. He knew that he had to master economics as that would be a key to understanding the world and then changing it for the better. He began to grapple with the subject of money and value, reading Smith and Ricardo and Malthus. Karl Marx had embarked on his life-long career of studying bourgeois society (not capitalism, as the word had still not been coined) in the hope of subverting it.[3]

In 1848 Europe was witnessing a political upheaval. With the spread of capitalism had come the desire for freedom. There were winds of radical change blowing through the old courts of European monarchies a mere three decades after they had defeated Napoleon and the French Revolution. France was yet again in the throes of an uprising. Another revolution seemed imminent.

That same year, sitting in a pub in Brussels during the last days of January and the first of February, two young men were hard at work to present their vision of what the revolution would be like. Friedrich Engels, just 28, was the son of a wealthy German industrialist and he had seen the Industrial Revolution at first hand when managing his father's factories in Manchester. Karl Marx was just two years his senior; Engels was convinced that Marx would be the leader of the movement to change the world. He was willing to bankroll him so that Marx could remain a journalist, a philosopher, a voracious reader of political economy and an agitator. He funded Marx's lifestyle for the rest of their lives together. The pamphlet they wrote made a trenchant commentary on the political economy of capitalism. They called it the bourgeois mode of production.

Their youthful pamphlet, *The Communist Manifesto*, became a classic of European political literature and was translated into virtually all the languages of the world. Even after 166 years, it makes fascinating reading and remains one of the best introductions to the global nature of capitalism. Marx and Engels saw capitalism not as a haven of static, tranquil equilibrium, but as a story of constant expansion and change accompanied by crises.

> Modern bourgeois society with its relations of production, of exchange and of property, a society that has conjured up such gigantic means of production and of exchange, is like the sorcerer, who is no longer able to control the powers of the nether world whom he has called up by his spells. ... It is enough to mention the commercial crises that by their periodic return put on its trial, each time more threateningly, the existence of the entire bourgeois society. In those crises a great part not only of the existing products, but also of the previously created productive forces, are periodically destroyed. In these crises there breaks out an epidemic that, in all earlier epochs, would have seemed an absurdity – the epidemic of overproduction. ... And how does the

bourgeoisie get over these crises? On the one hand by enforced destruction of a mass of productive forces; on the other, by the conquest of new markets, and by the more thorough exploitation of the old ones. That is to say, by paving the way for more extensive and more destructive crises, and by diminishing the means whereby crises are prevented.[4]

Of the two of them it was Engels who had first discovered the phenomenon of the crisis. While managing his father's Manchester factories, he had personally witnessed the distress. As he wrote in October 1847,

> The commercial crisis to which England finds itself exposed at the moment is, indeed, more severe than any of the preceding crises. Neither in 1837 nor in 1842 was the depression so universal as at the present time. All the branches of England's vast industry have been paralysed at the peak of its development; everywhere there is stagnation, everywhere one sees nothing but workers thrown out on the streets.[5]

The observation is clear. The crisis of 1847 was not an isolated instance. There had been similar episodes previously, in 1837 and 1842. Was this a recurrent pattern? Was there a systematic explanation for such crises? It was left to his friend Karl Marx, resuming his study of economics once the Revolution of 1848 had failed and embarking on 20 years of intense study, to come up with an answer.

As a trained philosopher yet an autodidact in economics, Marx mastered the labor theory of value and imbibed Ricardo's arguments. He wanted to prove that, just as Ricardo had argued that rent was an unproductive income accruing to landlords, profits were similarly unearned by the capitalist. They arose from the exploitation of workers. That done, he believed workers would revolt and overthrow capitalists.

It did not quite work out that way. Marx's ideas about the surplus value of the workers being the source of profits did not win many adherents. But what Marx did show, to his satisfaction and as a challenge to economists, was that booms and busts weren't accidental. Periods of high and low economic activity were a part of the way a capitalist economy functioned. Of course, he was writing nearly a century after Smith and half a century after Ricardo. The Industrial Revolution had spread much wider and entrenched itself in the British economy. In Smith's time, agriculture was predominant; now industry was. Workers had left their lands and were recruited into factories to work under "miserable conditions," an observation which his friend Engels had made about factories in Manchester in his 1845 book *The Condition of the Working Class in England*.

Marx could see that the growth of the industrial economy had made Adam Smith's invisible hand much more problematical than was thought originally. The economy worked through convulsions of crises, ups and downs rather than a smooth establishment of equilibrium. Some players – the capitalists for instance – could show more initiative than the workers, who depended on the capitalists to give them employment. Capitalists only gave work if they could make a profit by employing the workers. Exploiting workers and seizing the surplus value created by the workers was not enough for the capitalists. Their ability to realize profits, that is, convert surplus value into money, depended on the market for the goods they produced, which could be high or low depending on the interplay of different circumstances. For example, if a large number of capitalists were competing in the same market, they might produce more of a good than there was a demand for, which would cause the price of the good to fall. Instead of making profits they would be making losses. Or alternatively, if wages were too mean, then the workers would not be able to buy the goods produced and again losses would result. Capitalism was a dynamic disequilibrium order.

In *Das Kapital* (Capital), volume 1, Marx discerned a roughly ten-year cyclical pattern in British data.[6] Thus, in his view, the first crisis was in 1825. Other dates of rises are 1837–8, 1847, 1857, 1866. A crisis was just the turning point at which the boom collapses and the downward movement begins. Marx had a theory of why the cycles occurred and how they were essential, almost medicinal, for the working of the capitalist economy. For Marx, the basic mechanism of a capitalist economy was the search for profits which were then reinvested – accumulated – as capital. Profits and wages were two components of the total value added, defined as the value of the good over and above the value of the raw materials used up in production and the depreciation of equipment. Wages would be high in a boom since more labor was demanded relative to supply. But if wages were high, profits would suffer. If this tendency continued, then sooner or later the profit rate would decline and capitalists would feel threatened. At this juncture, some would go out of business and others would try to hire machinery which meant fewer workers were required. Hence the demand for labor would fall and the rise in wages would slow. As unemployment rose, wages would start to fall. Profits would rise. But with higher profits more capitalists would reenter the economy and this would boost the demand for workers. The wheel would turn again.

Marx had other theories for the cycles. Overproduction due to unbridled competition between producers, matched by a lack of demand due to low wages of workers which restricted demand, was another. Marxists went on debating many of his theories among themselves while mainstream economists were aware but skeptical of their validity.

Marx's theory of cycles is based on hypothesis about the "real" economy. In later volumes of *Capital* which he left unpublished during his lifetime, there are many discussions of financial crises, but they are not systematic. He did not explicitly weave in the role of financial markets in a theory of cycles. But many cycles from early days onward have had an element of financial panic or bank failures which trigger off the crisis. Financial crises and cycles became regular occurrences in Britain from the Battle of Waterloo onward.

A French physician, Clément Juglar, did some pioneering work in the measurement and analysis of cycles. Writing before Marx, he found ten-year cycles. Juglar abandoned his career as a physician in 1848 and took up their study. He published his classic account in 1860, *Des Crises commerciales et de leur retour périodique en France, en Angleterre, et aux États Unis* (Commercial crises and their recurrence in France, England and the United States). Juglar's theory of why crisis happened concerned monetary factors of credit creation and then withdrawal of credit by banks. (As we shall see below, the Swedish economist Knut Wicksell developed a similar theory.)

A crisis was a sudden turn in the market from boom to a collapse of prices and profits. What then followed was a long period of recession/depression before recovery and the resumption of boom. In Britain, crises occurred in 1816, 1825, 1836, 1847, 1857 and 1866, a year before Marx published the first volume of *Capital*. (At one stage in the late 1850s, Marx was seriously worried that capitalism might collapse before he had finished his critique of it!)

While the description of the crisis remained similar whether in 1825 or 1866, the financial markets had become much more sophisticated during the nineteenth century. There were many stocks (equities) and bonds which people bought and sold. Stock markets were perpetually active, with traders who relied on their intuition about risks and returns. Crises began in the stock markets and the markets for bonds and credit. While economists put money aside when discussing equilibrium, there was a steady growth of banks and the use of checks as the nineteenth century progressed. Banks began to cash checks for each other. This meant that the net settlement in terms of cash was often a fraction of the total amount written out in checks. Banks needed to keep a fraction of their total liabilities (the amount people had deposited with them) in cash and could lend the rest out to borrowers. These borrowers, in turn. did not withdraw cash but wrote checks against the amount credited to them as loans. The bank thus economized on cash and earned an interest on the loans they had made. The inverted pyramid of credit created on the base of cash could get steeper and steeper as the process of check clearing got quicker and more efficient. But, of course, there was a risk of overlending and being caught short of cash when depositors demanded their cash back. Often, if there was a rumor that a bank was in trouble, depositors would rush to get their cash out and this in itself would drive the bank to a closure.

It was in such an atmosphere of hectic activity that in 1866 the Bank of England was called upon to save a City of London bank – Overend & Gurney – which was under the threat of bankruptcy. The Bank of England decided that it would lend cash of its own to save a supplicant bank if there was on offer some "sound paper" – loans which had been given which could be recovered, investments made which could be cashed. Thus was born the idea of the Bank of England – a Central Bank – as a "lender of the last resort." The Bank of England, although still a private company, became the supervisory agent which regulated the behavior of commercial banks. Banks agreed to leave some of their cash with the Bank of England as reserves, as the Bank of England was financially stable. In 1890, the Bank of England was required to intervene once again when Baring Brothers, a bank with investments in Latin America, was caught short of liquidity. This was a crisis of globalization. Again the Bank of England was able to cope.

By the turn of the nineteenth century, a variety of financial instruments had been devised in which people could invest their spare cash. They could lend money on the overnight market in which banks borrowed cash, or buy 90-day bills. Traders issued these bills to get cash to pay their suppliers before the sale of goods brought them some cash back. Their suppliers, who received the bills, went to the banks, which cashed them for a small discount. Banks then collected the bills when they matured.

Companies issued shares under limited liability rules. Governments and some larger companies issued bonds. There was a thriving market in agricultural mortgages for farmers and a smaller one in residential mortgages, which were required by the relatively better-off middle classes. Often entrepreneurs would have schemes for launching new products, raising money by issuing shares or bonds. Financial assets multiplied. Railroads were financed this way. The share prices of railroads rose and fell as their prospects fluctuated. Financial markets became central to the growth of national economies, with many specialized players and thousands of ordinary participants.

Central to the functioning of the financial markets was the idea that the higher the risk, the higher would be the return the issuer had to offer. The return on any asset was driven by the expectations of its future yield and hence subject to the psychological forces of manias and panics. At the base was cash, the safest asset but with zero yield, and at the farthest point was investment in some future prospect of untold riches touted by an entrepreneur. The more developed the financial market, the longer the distance between ready cash and the most profitable asset available. One could have bonds or equities or mortgages, and in more modern times derivatives, which are based on equities and which figured so largely in the equitized subprime mortgage crisis. Central Banks were there to ensure that the credit was sound. Governments had to make sure that the money they issued was sound as well. Their coins would be based on gold convertibility, and the notes issued in their name, or in the name of the bank authorized to issue them, such as the Bank of England, were also issued in proper quantities, neither over-issued nor under-issued. But, of course, real life was never that simple.

The International Gold Standard was adopted by country after country wanting to be able to borrow money from abroad. Convertibility of a currency in terms of gold was a guarantee that it would never be over-issued since people could change it for gold. Once you had a sound currency, you could attract capital from abroad as well as from local investors. France was able to float government debt soon after Waterloo when the Bourbon kings were restored to the throne. This gave confidence in the government's credit and English investors, including David Ricardo, bought the French debt just as Dutch and German investors did. The Rothschilds opened their London office just on the eve of the Battle of Waterloo. Britain went back to Gold Standard six years after its victory. The withdrawal of the paper currency created much hardship, as we saw above, as prices fell and workers lost their jobs. Debts incurred in happier times when prices were high now had to be paid back when prices were low.

Similar events occurred in the United States when the greenbacks issued by the North during the Civil War were withdrawn after it ended. The US wanted to prove its creditworthiness and joined the Gold Standard in 1873. The process led to distress among the farmers who had taken out mortgages during the inflationary period of the war. Repayment was difficult as the prices of agricultural produce were falling with the expansion of international trade thanks to better ships. Now Australia and New Zealand supplied Europe just as well as America could. The result was a long downward cycle of agricultural prices from 1873 to 1896

The businessmen – owners of railroads and steel companies – wanted to attract capital from Europe and they supported sound money. The battle between the interests of the farmers and the moneymen was echoed in the famous cry of William Jennings Bryan, thrice presidential candidate, "You shall not hang Mankind on the Cross of Gold." Despite being a good orator, he never won any of the three elections he contested.

It was the growth of banking and the proliferation of financial instruments that were creating a new environment by the second half of the nineteenth century. If in Marx's time the capitalist could be called "Mr. Moneybags," now it was access to bank credit which drove investment. Thus the monetary context of the late nineteenth-century economy was different from that of Marx's time. It fell to a Swedish economist, Knut Wicksell, to propose a theory of cycles to suit those times.

The Trouble Maker

Knut Wicksell (1851–1926) was a controversial figure in his day. He was a Malthusian and advocated birth control. He was suspected of being an atheist and an anti-royalist, and was sent to jail for two months for satirizing the Immaculate Conception. Trained as a mathematician, he became attracted to economics when attending lectures given by Carl Menger at the University of Vienna. Wicksell was a socialist and aware of Marx's work. Fascinated by the moneyless equilibrium theories of Ricardo and Walras, he took on the task of reconciling these with the messy world of money and financial crises.

Wicksell hypothesized that if the equilibrium theory of Ricardo and Walras was true, as he believed it to be, yet cycles occurred in the real world, the explanation for the difference between the two must be an element which was missing in the theory but was present in real life. The missing link he proposed was money and credit.[7] In pure theory, the acts of demand and supply, of consumption and production, take place instantaneously, or at least without any need for credit or money. But real life entrepreneurs borrowed money to buy inputs and pay their workers and only repaid the loans when they sold their output. Marx had also noticed this problem, and referenced it in the second volume of *Capital*, where he stated that money was converted into money capital when the capitalist invested the money in production. The capitalist then reconverted the output into money and realized his profits or losses, as the case may be. But the entire process took time. It was dynamic, unlike the instant equilibrium of Ricardo and Walras. Marx, however, did not integrate his theory of cycles with his theory of money. It was Wicksell who was to attempt the task.

Wicksell began by contrasting the rate of interest at which banks were willing to lend money – the market rate of interest – and the rate of profit the borrower could make if he invested the money – the natural rate of interest. Of course, the notion of profits had been eliminated from economic theory. Marx had talked about profitability and the declining rate of profit, etc. Profits had somehow become a dirty word for economic theorists. (It was Hayek who conjectured that Wicksell renamed the rate of profit the natural rate.) So Wicksell defined the natural rate as the rate at which savings and investment would equilibrate in a barter economy where money played no part. Money was irrelevant to the natural rate and hence it could be part of a Walrasian economy. Of course, in a real economy the rates would be expressed as being paid out in money. Money is here just a unit of account and a device for making payments. It does not play an active role in a Walrasian economy. But in an actual economy, money plays an important, and often by implication a disturbing role when it comes to causing cycles.

If the market rate was below the natural rate, then borrowers would happily borrow, as they stood to make profits. This started off a boom which could go on in a cumulative fashion, but sooner or later bankers lost their nerve or found many more people coming back for cash than they had made provision for. So they would hike up the market rate. Soon some borrowers would begin to make losses. Demand for loans would diminish. The economy would reverse from an upswing to a downswing, which would be cumulative as well.

It was the fact that banks cleared each other's checks which allowed a large credit structure to be built up above a small cash base. But eventually cash was needed to meet the demands of depositors, including the few who wanted ready cash rather than a check. So the banking system was at the root of the phenomenon of cycles. What Wicksell did not have was a theory of the turning point, the point at which the boom stopped and the economy turned downward. But he did provide a theory of cycles in an economy using money. Thus we have equilibrium market theories of Ricardo and Walras along with Wicksell's theory of cycles – which more or less is still the basic theory around which many economists work. Even the current crisis can be understood in Wicksellian terms.

There is thus a division within economics as to how to perceive the economy. Is the economy a system which tends to an equilibrium almost all of the time, or is it a system which tends to disequilibrium and cyclical fluctuations? The tradition of Ricardo and Walras takes the equilibrium route. The equilibrium tradition is the more dominant one, especially in recent years. The tradition of Marx and Wicksell takes the disequilibrium path. And there are insights in the disequilibrium tradition which can be illuminating.

It was Joseph Schumpeter who gave economics not only a theory but a vision – *weltanschauung* – about how capitalism flourished through a series of cycles of booms and busts.

Creative Destruction

The second half of the nineteenth century witnessed one of the many episodes of globalization. This one was built on the industrial and financial revolutions. The new inventions in transport and communications – railroads, steamships and the introduction of the telegraph – had connected the many parts of the world. International trade had knitted together the world economy, spanning the Americas to the Antipodes and all continents in between. Workers migrated from Europe to North and South America, from India to Africa and the Caribbean, from China to America and other parts of Asia and Africa. The years 1873 to 1896 are labeled the Great Depression as prices of agricultural products fell steadily. (Modern economic historians are skeptical about the label.) Economic growth was steady, however, across Europe and the US. Thanks to the falling prices of food items, the workers' living standards improved even as unemployment fell and rose in cycles. The financial revolution enabled cities in South America to raise capital for building railways and tramways on the London stock market. But there were victims too. Baring Brothers narrowly avoided collapse, saved only by the speed with which the Bank of England reacted. The US attracted a lot of European capital as it expanded westward after the Civil War and also received a large influx of workers from Europe.

The ideas of Marx were gaining support in the workers' movements, if not in the halls of academia. The First Socialist International had been founded by Marx in 1864 but it lasted only until 1871. In 1889 the Second International was founded, and despite many breakaways the Socialist International is still around. Socialist movements in Germany and France adhered to Marx's ideas about the problems of capitalism. A determined answer to Marx's theory of profits as surplus value was given by the Austrian economist Eugene von Böhm-Bawerk, who pointed out some logical inconsistencies in the argument. But the only economist to take up Marx's challenge of explaining the dynamics of capitalism was another Austrian, a student of Böhm-Bawerk.

Joseph Schumpeter (1883–1950) studied economics in Vienna but his ambition was to be the best horseman, the best lover, as well as the best economist of his generation. He claimed to have achieved two out of the three ambitions, though we don't know which they were. Rather like Ricardo, he was a busy man of affairs as he became Finance Minister in Austria for a while and dabbled in stock markets till he finally became Professor of Economics at Harvard. He wrote a two-volume treatise on *Business Cycles* in 1939 and a masterly *History of Economic Analysis*, which was published posthumously.

But his best-known book was the one he wrote when he was only 30 years old. *The Theory of Economic Development* is a book which breaks the mold of economic theory from the static equilibrium visions of Ricardo and Walras. Schumpeter gave an explanation of what made capitalism the dynamic disequilibrium system it is, and indeed he thought he could refute and improve upon Marx as he expounded his theory. He saw capitalism as subject to long cycles of boom and bust, cycles which could last 50 years. But these cycles were evidence of the creativity, albeit the destructive creativity, of capitalism. Each cycle was set off by a cluster of innovations. Railroads would be one example. Innovations were the clever exploitation of existing ideas in technology which were waiting to be exploited for profit. Only an entrepreneur, a word rarely used until Schumpeter chose it to represent a special type of businessman, would have the vision to spot the potential gain. Ferdinand de Lesseps, who saw the potential of the Suez Canal, would be one such entrepreneur. Bill Gates in our day is another. Once an entrepreneur had launched an innovation, there would be followers and competitors who would add to the tide of investment. Most such investments were financed by borrowings from shareholders or banks. The payoff was not immediate but when it came, it was massive. The innovation transformed the economy, with many larger repercussions in sectors other than where it started. Thus railroads changed not only the cost of transport but the way people could build communities, resulting in urbanization with cities and towns. The boom set off by the innovation would last a while and then the excess profits would begin to dry up. The imitators would cut the margins of profit and a downturn would follow until another innovation occurred. Toward the end of the nineteenth century, roughly 50 years after the invention of the railroads, came the innovations in chemicals, electricity, telephones and automobiles, and bunched simultaneously they sparked another cycle. Silicon Valley characterized the innovation cluster in our day.

New technology displaced old technology and destroyed many old jobs. Railroads displaced canals and horse carriages. In a previous cluster, textile factories destroyed cottage spinning and weaving, iron and steel factories made blacksmiths unnecessary. The Luddites who attacked machinery in England in the early nineteenth century were expressing a fear of new technology which has never gone away. But Schumpeter saw that each wave of innovations reconfigures the economy and creates new jobs. However, this is done not in the neat and tidy fashion of the market reaching equilibrium, but through booms and busts. Capitalism would lose its dynamism if this process was somehow interfered with. Even so, the theories of Marx and Schumpeter or the measurements of Juglar remained to be validated by extensive quantitative research using new methods of analyzing time series of economic data and a modicum of mathematical modeling.

This was to happen along with the growth of econometrics in mid-twentieth century, as we shall see in a later chapter.

The Long and Short

When the Russian Revolution occurred in October 1917 it looked as if Marx's ideas and his prophecies were valid. Of course, the prediction had been that a revolution would come in a mature capitalist country. When it came, it would be triggered by a deep crisis in the system. Marxists were thus fascinated by the study of cycles and their intensity. They believed crises would get progressively more intense till the "final crisis" which would lead to the collapse of capitalism, followed by a workers' revolution. Mature economies had interconnections and would drag each other into a common crisis led by the most advanced capitalist country: Great Britain, for example. The revolution instead came in Russia, which was still a developing economy. But capitalism did not decline.

Lenin, the leader of the Russian Revolution, was wedded to Marx's ideas. He encouraged a boom in the study of cycles. A Russian economist, Nikolai Dimitrievich Kondratieff (1892–1931), analyzed the data available up to the end of World War I and concluded that he could spot long cycles of 40 to 60 years.[8] Kondratieff had been influential as a young economist before the Russian Revolution when he briefly became a minister in the last non-Communist government Russia had had. He had studied under Michael Tugan-Baranowsky, a famous Russian

Marxist. After the Revolution, Kondratieff taught and later established an Institute for Konjunktur, that is, the study of business cycles, Konjunktur being the German expression for cycles. He published his ideas in 1925 while there was a liberal and open atmosphere in Russia. But when Stalin came into power in 1927, the liberal atmosphere ended. Kondratieff was punished for his ideas. If capitalism can have regular cycles of 50 or 60 years, it can never end and the hope of the Communist revolutionaries that an end to capitalism would come after a final crisis would be negated. He was sent to the Gulag and died in 1931. His ideas remain suggestive, though debatable, as we shall see below.

Kondratieff 's theory of the long cycles combines economic and political variables. Thus demographic variables, the long gestation period before investments in durable goods bear fruit (shipbuilding, for example), and often political upheavals (wars and revolutions) may delay or hasten turning points. The chronology of the long cycles established by Kondratieff was as follows:

> First long wave upswing 1780s–1810/17; downswing 1810/ 17–1844/51
>
> Second long wave upswing 1844/51–1870/75; downswing 1870/75–1890/96
>
> Third long wave upswing 1890/96–1914/20; downswing 1914/20–?

Kondratieff left the cycle dating unfinished as he was writing in the 1920s. But one can see that the downswing of 1914/20 lasted till 1940/45. We can extend his calculations tentatively as follows:

Fourth long wave upswing 1940/45–1970/75; downswing 1970/75–1990/95

Fifth long wave upswing 1990/95–2005/10; downswing 2005/10–?

The cycles are thus long but not of uniform length. Shorter cycles of three to four years or Marx-type cycles of ten years would be interwoven in these long cycles. The dates are suggestive rather than precise. Even so Kondratieff's ideas are not without merit. Given that the data can discern no more than four or five waves, statistical precision is out of the question. The sample is just too small. But combining Schumpeter's ideas of innovation clusters with demographic and political factors, one can begin to use Kondratieff's theories as a rough guide to the idea that we live in a system where one should never believe that the good times, or indeed the miserable times, will last forever.

The remarkable fact about the Kondratieff concept is the similarity of the dates between the nineteenth and the twentieth centuries, especially in the seventies of both centuries where a turning point comes which takes the economy from prosperity into a downturn. As I show later, in Chapter 5, Ernest Mandel, a Belgian Marxist, was able to use his reading of the cyclical literature to express doubts that the Keynesian boom of the post-World War II period would continue. He pinpointed the 1970s as the likely date of its reversal. This is a rare example of the heuristic way in which such theory can be of use.

The tradition in which Marx, Juglar and even Schumpeter worked was an empirical one but it lacked the support of modern statistical methods. These methods have much improved the way we think of the data on income, employment, prices and other variables that are now increasingly available. The development of these methods and the logical way of thinking about cycles had a great boost during the early decades of the twentieth century, but that will be discussed in its proper place.

Chapter Three

NEW TOOLS FOR A NEW PROFESSION

Alfred Marshall and the Professionalization of Economics

Adam Smith was a Professor of Moral Philosophy and David Ricardo a stockbroker. Thomas Robert Malthus was the first economist paid to teach the subject at Haileybury College, established by the East India Company to prepare its employees before they went to India. But Malthus apart, economics was not a profession which could be practiced by writers on economics such as John Stuart Mill. By the 1870s economics had become a professional subject. Walras was appointed as a Professor of Economics at Lausanne, and his two contemporaries Jevons and Menger were also Professors of Political Economy. But the person with whom the professionalization of economics, and indeed the change in the name of the subject from political

economy to economics, is most associated is Alfred Marshall
(1842–1924).

While professor at the University of Cambridge, Marshall
wrote his magnum opus, *Principles of Economics*. It was to became
the standard text for economics, used for decades after its first
publication in 1890; its content still serves as the basic curriculum for teaching economics. The text itself went through eight
editions between 1890 and 1920.

Marshall's wife, Mary, was one of the first women graduates
of Cambridge University and co-authored a book with her
husband on *The Economics of Industry*. Their home received
numerous undergraduates and fellow economists over the years
the Marshalls lived in Cambridge.

Alfred Marshall had the energy and spirit to fight academic
battles in Cambridge. Through his skirmishes he carved out a
separate space for economics – downplaying the importance of
history, even economic history, in the economics curriculum. He
created an Economics Tripos degree at Cambridge, the first of its
kind, which gave students the opportunity to specialize in
economics. This model was copied across many English-speaking
universities within the British Empire and in the US as well.

Marshall built up the basic corpus of economics as it came to
be taught. He had the clever idea of using mathematics in his
arguments but hiding it in the footnotes and appendices. He
translated his mathematical results in lugubrious prose and
pretended that he was writing for the practical businessman.
Nothing was to be stated too elegantly or with mathematical

precision, even if it was precise. Marshall deployed the ambigui-
ties of the English language as his secret weapon. Demand and
supply, capital and labor, rent and profits, international trade –
all were discussed in prose. Marshall did harness geometry and
translated many of the otherwise algebraic propositions of
economic theory into geometry as two-dimensional diagrams.
This gave economics an elegant scientific look and diagrams
became the staple instrument for the exposition of economics.

Marshall's greatest legacy is the iconic Marshallian Cross.
This is the diagram of a demand curve sloping downward from
left to right and the supply curve sloping upward from right to
left (see Figure 1). The two axes are price as the vertical axis and
quantity demanded/supplied as the horizontal axis. (To begin
with, Marshall had the axes the other way around but this was
reversed later by other economists.) At the point of intersection
equilibrium is determined and at this point you can read off the
price at which the transactions will be carried out and the quantity which will be bought. At a price above equilibrium more is
supplied than demanded and at a price below equilibrium more
is demanded than supplied. To reach equilibrium, price has to
be lowered when the supply exceeds the demand and vice versa
when supply falls short. Generations of students would learn
their basic economics from that diagram. It is carved on the glass
doors at the entrance of one of the buildings at the London
School of Economics (LSE).

The works of Walras and Menger were familiar to Marshall.
Avoiding the gross impracticalities of general equilibrium, he

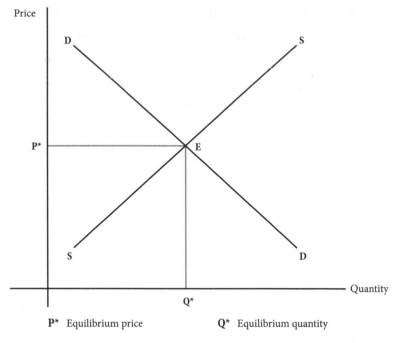

Price

P*

S   D

Q*

Quantity

P* Equilibrium price   **Q*** Equilibrium quantity

Figure 1 Marshall's Cross

took one market at a time and discussed how an equilibrium price would be established. This was partial equilibrium. He distinguished between commodities where supply could adjust quickly to demand and those where the adjustment would take time. He introduced the role of time in a cautious fashion, without using mathematics.

Thus, on any day, the market would determine price depending on how much was demanded and how much was supplied. Take the market for strawberries, for example. In the time before refrigeration had been invented, at the end of every day the unsold strawberries would be thrown away. But this was just a very short period. If you examined prices over a week you had more stability, and a year would allow supply to adjust much better. For a durable good such as housing, the adjustments would take much longer and prices would be volatile. But it could all be encompassed in the notion of equilibrium.

Marshall taught the growth of firms and the expansion of whole industries in the same gentle prose he used to explain how the price of tea was determined. Economics was to be a useful subject dealing with the daily business of life. And yet behind this easy facade was the certainty that whatever the economic problem, the answer could be readily found. English-speaking economists stopped reading German or French books. It was the heyday of the British Empire and it seemed easy to say "It is all in Marshall."

Marshall made the ideas of marginal and average costs familiar to economists. He established that the most efficient outcome for a firm was where the marginal cost of producing a good equaled its price. Competition between many small firms producing an identical product (farmers of wheat, for example) would result in an identical price for every producer/seller and in the end profits would be minimal thanks to competition. A monopoly, on the other hand, would drive a wedge between marginal cost and price and yield excess profits. Marshall gave a practical business air to economics.

Adam Smith and all those who wrote in his tradition believed in the desirability of free movement of capital and labor between different sectors and the unrestricted movement of goods internationally. Marshall gave this idea a precise form by formulating a theory of competition. In a competitive industry, all firms would be small and none would be able to dominate the market. Firms would be "price takers" rather than "price setters." They would maximize profits if each equated its marginal cost to the price. The maximum profit might well be zero or at most "normal" with no "excess" profits accruing to any firm. Each firm had some fixed costs and some costs which varied with the quantity of output produced. As production started, average costs fell because the burden of fixed costs fell per unit of output. But eventually the variable cost component would come to dominate and average cost would rise. The best point at which to stop production would be when average costs were at their minimum. This was also by a happy mathematical accident the point at which marginal cost equaled average cost, and, of course, price equaled marginal cost. As price equaled average cost at this point, profits were zero! This is the point of maximum efficiency for the firm. If competition prevailed everywhere in the economy, all firms would produce at their minimum average costs and the economy would be at its maximum efficiency. Even today in formulating policy, we try to enforce rules of competition such that no firm can have excessive market power. (An interesting consequence of this conjecture is that if all firms produced at the lowest point of the U-shaped average cost curve, one would never find a U-shaped cost curve in the data but only the left half of the U.)

Economic reality was, of course, that large industrial firms were emerging with the ability to earn "increasing returns" or economies of scale. A steel factory would be feasible only at a high level of output and its average costs would go on declining over a wide range of output. This was because the fixed – capital – costs of starting a steel factory are very high and the variable costs – raw materials and labor – are relatively lower. The rules of the competitive firm would not carry across. There would be only a few firms providing steel in any economy and each could wield some market power. These issues led later to the development of theories of imperfect competition and monopolistic competition, where the price would be above the marginal cost and production would not be at least cost. The modern-day equivalents are the gas and electricity companies. The market is limited to a few players by the high fixed costs involved in setting up an energy company.

It was in the US that there was great concern about cartels and trusts – large companies capable of wielding market power. The railroad companies had often collaborated with the large industrial firms to shut out smaller competitors. Pricing by these large firms showed monopoly power. The US was going through a period of rapid growth but agricultural prices fell between 1873 and 1913. There was large-scale immigration from Europe and wages were not growing fast. In this atmosphere there was a strong political movement – the Progressive Movement, which during the last decade of the nineteenth century and the first decade of the twentieth fought cartels and trusts. The US had the first legislation for constraining market power – the Clayton Act and the Sherman Act. Trust-busting remained a much stronger theme in American political economy than was the case in Europe. Marshall mentioned monopolies but did not see them as a major problem in the modern economy.

Marshall was a reconciler. The change from the old economics of Smith and Ricardo, "classical economics," to the marginalist theories of Walras, Jevons and Menger was quite sharp. Marshall coined the expression "neoclassical economics" to discourage any idea of a rupture in the discipline. The theory of prices became for economists the core of microeconomics. The world had to wait for the birth of macroeconomics as a formal part of economics.

The Quantity Theory of Money

Marshall never wrote the great book which was to cover the aspects of money and the economy as a whole. But he did start a train of thought which was most fruitful. Economists from Locke onward had asserted that the more money there was in the economy, the higher prices would be. This was later formulated by a physicist Simon Newcomb as the "equation of exchange":

$$MV = PT$$

M is the stock of money in the economy, V its velocity. Together they give us an estimate of how much purchasing power is sloshing around in the economy. P is the general price level and T the volume of transactions. If there is too much money M, or if it circulates faster – higher V – then for any given volume of transactions T the price level P will rise. If velocity V is constant, then there is a direct relation between money M and price level P given transactions T.

Irving Fisher (1867–1947) made the first attempt to measure the variables M, V, P, T from American data.[1] Every purchase involves a monetary counterpart. Many purchases are of perishable commodities but others are of existing durable assets – houses, for example. So if all the transactions can be measured in any one period – say in a year – then we can derive the composite measure PT, which will be the total value of money transactions. The next step is to construct a general price index P from the data for the various things bought and sold and then T can be derived from that. Using bank data we can work out how much money has been in circulation during the year and derive the velocity V as well.

The logic of the quantity theory is that the velocity will be constant or change relatively slowly. Thus the ratio of the money stock M to the volume of transactions T will tell us about the price level. The higher M is relative to T, the higher will be P.

The truth of this equation is often asserted as the only valid result of economics, or, for the skeptics, a meaningless identity which is true only because the definitions of the various components make it so. Either way, the question is: How does money affect the economic system? With the theory of individual prices derived without any reference to money, what is the transmission mechanism by which money raises all prices?

85

Marshall in his own deliberately imprecise way gave an answer. Every individual or household always carried a certain portion of its income or wealth or property in the form of a ready cash balance. This was because money was useful for purchases, good to have for a rainy day, and crucial if you saw a bargain which you wanted to snap up. Having money at hand was good for all these three reasons. Later they were described as the three motives for holding money: transactions, precautionary and speculative.

Arthur Cecil Pigou (1877–1959), who succeeded Marshall as Professor of Economics at Cambridge, formulated this idea into an equation. But he also adapted it to the case of individuals holding bank deposits as a form of alternative to ready cash.

$$M = kPA\left[c + b\left(1 - c\right)\right]$$

M is the amount of money the household wishes to hold, P is price level, and A the real income of the household. The proportion c is held in the form of cash and b is the banking system's reserve cash ratio, and so $(1 - c)$ is held by the public as bank deposits. The same equation holds at the aggregate level because each side could be added up across households. k is the constant fraction of income the household wants to have in cash. Thus a household may keep one quarter of its income in cash and three-quarters in the bank. Then c is 0.25. The advantage of this formulation is that it proposes a theory of economic behavior of the household regarding money. It defines the demand for money at the household level, which can then be taken to be valid at the level of the economy (provided we assume that the constant k is the same across all households).[2] Later, John Maynard Keynes, who was to be the most famous student of Marshall and Pigou, developed this idea further. His work was to revolutionize economics. But that is for later.

The Messenger of Market Failure

The steady growth and low inflation of the last 40 years of the nineteenth century had brought prosperity to the skilled working classes of Europe. Even the unskilled had benefited from cheap food. Yet the more Europe prospered, the more the problems of economic growth surfaced. Factories were spewing smoke and polluting rivers. London was often blanketed in a thick smog when the weather turned bad, leaving the poorer inhabitants of the city vulnerable to respiratory and other infectious diseases. The "dark satanic mills" William Blake had denounced were very much a fact of life. New social forces were arising in prosperous economies that wanted to correct these defects. Trade unions were on the rise and beginning to fight the cause of unskilled and semiskilled workers. Rich philanthropists such as Charles Booth and Seebohm Rowntree had discovered the poverty in urban England. The Liberal Party, once a party with an aristocratic leadership embracing orthodox finance, morphed into a fighting machine for reforms at home and liberal intervention abroad.

It was in this context that Alfred Marshall's successor, Arthur Cecil Pigou, pioneered the subject of welfare economics. Up until this juncture, government interventions were considered harmful, if not positively ruinous, if they were employed for more than a temporary period. Pigou, however, began to explore areas where the market failed to deliver the best outcomes and state intervention would allow the prices to adjust to their natural level if market failure had not occurred.[3]

Pigou formulated the notion of externality. This was the effect of one person's consumption, or one factory's production, on others. Thus the smoke spewed out by a factory harmed the health of people living in the neighborhood and imposed a cost, such as medical expenses. But this cost was not reflected in the total cost of producing the good. The factory was making a profit but only by exporting the true costs to others. To reflect the true costs of production, and to recover the cost that had been imposed on others, the factory had to be taxed. The market in this instance had failed to reflect the true – social – cost and so the market failure had to be corrected. Only the state had the neutral authority to impose such taxes. Conversely, if an activity was indirectly beneficial, then the government would award subsidies.

Pigou made a breach in the classical and neoclassical idea that the market knew best and left to itself would produce the best of outcomes. Even so, Pigou did not reject the market and its benefits. His purpose was to make the market a better instrument with which to maximize the welfare of the people. Pigou gave governments the tools to intervene in a market for the purpose of improving its performance. His insights have now been extended to many human activities. The most prominent example of the use of externalities has been in relation to carbon emissions.

Pigou's breach paved the way for the idea that for markets to work efficiently they have to be underpinned with strong regulation. In the wake of the financial crisis, legislators have returned to the task of making financial regulation tighter and imposing conditions on bank behavior so that the interests of depositors and taxpayers are protected.

The Great War and the End of the Steadily Growing Economy

The hundred years between the Battle of Waterloo and the outbreak of World War I were regarded as a tranquil period in Western Europe – Pax Britannica. Of course, elsewhere Europeans had built empires, colonizing peoples of Asia and Africa. In the Western hemisphere, Europeans had displaced old civilizations and built new countries. In North America, the republic of the United States and the colonial settlement of Canada grew up as countries with capitalism and liberty, while Mexico went through multiple convulsions before it, too, became a republic. In South America, the nations had oligarchies based on landed property, whether in minerals or agriculture. Either way, through the long century of peace in Western Europe, the Western hemisphere was an additional source of growth – of raw material supplies and demand for capital.

The notion of a steadily growing economy or a smooth equilibrium was not fanciful if you were among the better-off bourgeoisie of Western Europe. A gentleman was defined as someone who did not have to work. A member of the rentier class, he had an income of a thousand pounds derived from the dividends of what he or his parents had invested in. Prices had been steady or falling. Inflation became a forgotten phenomenon, relegated to the past. Thrift was rewarded. The Gold Standard kept countries on a tight leash, enforcing balanced budgets and a money supply beyond manipulation by governments. The Bank of England acquired a prestige, unequaled since, as the benign regulator of the global economy. All was well in the best of all possible worlds.

As Keynes put it in his controversial book *The Economic Consequences of the Peace,*

The inhabitant of London could order by telephone, sipping his morning tea in bed, the various products of the whole earth, in such quantities as he might see fit, and reasonably expect their early delivery upon his doorstep; he could at the same moment and by the same means adventure his wealth in the natural resources and new enterprises of any quarter of the world, and share without exertion or even trouble, in their prospective fruits and advantages; or he could decide to couple the security of his fortunes with the good faith of the townspeople of any substantial municipality in any continent that fancy or information might recommend. He could secure forthwith, if he wished it, cheap and comfortable means of transit to any country or climate without passport or other formality, could dispatch his servant to the neighbouring office of a bank for such supply of the precious metals as might seem convenient, and could then proceed abroad to foreign quarters, without knowledge of their religion, language, or customs, bearing coined wealth upon his person, and would consider himself greatly aggrieved and much surprised at the least interference.[4]

This world was shattered by the outbreak of the war. It was the first Great War, with vast armies recruited from civilian populations and mechanized warfare. In its four years, millions died in Europe and economic life was never the same again. The war was expensive. Britain abandoned the Gold Standard for the duration of the war much as it had done in 1797 during the Anglo-French War. To negate the adverse impacts of losing large swathes of the male populace to the war effort, women were, controversially, recruited into the workforce. The principal combatants – Britain, Germany, the Austro-Hungarian Empire, the Ottoman Empire, France and Russia – suffered a lot of economic damage and loss of population. Russia witnessed a revolution which rejected capitalism and embarked upon the experiment of building a communist society on principles other than those of the market and private property. Germany was ruined and punished with the payment of a large reparations bill to the victorious allies. The Austro-Hungarian Empire, which had lasted for centuries, dissolved into many separate nations. The Ottoman Empire was partitioned, with Turkey emerging as a powerful military nation under Mustafa Kemal Atatürk. The remaining territories of the empire – what we now know as the Middle East – became attached to Britain or France on a "caretaker" basis. The US emerged as the most powerful economy at the end of the war. A late entrant to the war on the Allied side, and with the fighting taking place in Europe, it had suffered very little material loss. It became the creditor nation with the largest stock of gold in its coffers, while all European combatants were debtors.

Britain abandoned the Gold Standard again, along with most other European countries, and did not return to it until 1925. Since the Gold Standard was predicated on converting currencies at the rate implied by the gold content of the currency, there was no theory of how one currency should be exchanged against another if their values were not fixed in terms of gold.

Gustav Cassel (1866–1945) was the economist who proposed a theory of foreign exchange rates. His idea was rooted in the quantity theory of money. The rate at which two currencies would exchange, according to his theory, was determined by the purchasing power of each currency within its country of circulation. If one were to take an identical basket of commodities and compare how much it would cost in terms of each currency in the two countries, then the ratio was the correct rate of exchange. This was called the purchasing power parity (PPP) theory. Thus, if a basket filled with the same goods cost $350 to purchase in the US and £100 to purchase in the UK, the exchange rate would be $3.50 to the pound. If prices in the UK rose faster than in the US, and the same two baskets now cost £175 and $350 respectively, the new exchange rate would be $2.00 to the pound. The pound would have depreciated against the US dollar since one pound now bought only $2.00 rather than $3.50.

The theory does not envisage the modern practices of trading in foreign exchange instruments where the rate of interest that, say, a dollar asset would yield relative to a sterling asset would also enter into the exchange rate consideration. In a fully globalized world with no barriers to trade or movements of capital – an economist's ideal world – economic theory suggests that the real interest rates (nominal interest rate less the rate of inflation) will have a tendency to be equal. Thus, if a gap was to open up between the interest rate of any particular asset, say a bond, as between two markets, it would create opportunities for traders to arbitrage – buy in the cheap market and sell in the expensive one. This would eventually restore the equality of real interest rates. This is known as real interest parity.

The first practical demonstration of Cassel's theory was provided in Britain when debating the rate at which the pound should return to the Gold Standard.[5] The Great War had transformed the British economy. For one thing it had eliminated any unemployment; if anything, there was a chronic labor shortage, a situation unknown through the "century of peace." Trade unions had become powerful as their cooperation was sought to fight the war. When the war ended the British economy witnessed the return of something it had not experienced since before the Battle of Waterloo – inflation. Wage demands reached 20 percent plus for the successive years 1919 and 1920.

Wholesale prices rose 40 percent over two years. The British economy, which had been at full capacity through the war and had been growing healthily in the two decades prior to it, suddenly slumped and output declined by 20 percent over the same two years during which the prices rose. There had to be a drastic cutback in government spending (the so-called Geddes Axe named after the civil servant who proposed the cuts), which plunged the economy into a year which saw a 20 percent fall in the price level as well as in output. From then on, the British economy struggled to recover its pre-1914 prosperity. Along the way, economics was challenged to come up with new ideas to cope with the new reality and to find ways to nudge the economy back on to the path of prosperity.

Budgets had to be balanced again. The debt incurred during the war had to be serviced, adding to public spending. There was a need for "retrenchment," as public spending cuts were then called. Returning to the Gold Standard was also high on the agenda. Orthodox opinion in the Bank of England and the City of London favored going back at the old parity of $4.86 to the pound. John Maynard Keynes (1883–1946) pointed out in a series of articles, which later became his book *A Tract on Monetary Reform*, that, given the movement of wholesale prices in the UK and US, it would be better to fix the exchange rate at a lower level. Despite a year of severe deflation, the two postwar years of inflation had kept prices permanently above their prewar level. Going back at the old parity would mean an overvalued pound which would make British exports uncompetitive. Data on wholesale price movements were becoming available on a regular basis for a number of countries. This allowed Keynes to illustrate his argument with British and American wholesale price indices.

Keynes was ignored and Britain went back to the Gold Standard at the old parity. The decision proved disastrous and led to economic stagnation and labor strife in Britain in the second half of the 1920s. On the continent, Germany had been burdened with a large reparations demand. When it faltered, France moved in troops and occupied the Ruhr area where coal and other resources could be seized. Germany in return tried to highlight its distress by sabotaging its currency – inflating its prices so much that one needed millions of marks to buy a loaf of bread. Workers were paid twice a day, with the wage rising during the day to compensate for the hyperinflation. Nothing could be done to stem the tide of hyperinflation except to suspend the old currency, postpone the reparations payment and arrange loans for Germany from the only creditor nation remaining – the US.

The US was the only economy that was prospering. Indeed, it had its upswing in the 1920s – the Roaring Twenties – with a booming stock market and rising consumer demand marred only by Prohibition. These were the years of jazz and the flappers and the Great Gatsby. Russia suffered from a civil war and famine, but by the mid-1920s the Communist Party had consolidated its rule, and by late 1920s it had embarked on a program of planned development.

The Great Depression

The world's strongest economy also proved to be its weak spot. The US economy had been on a growth trajectory but there was also financial excess. The stock market had had a bull run for nine years. Many amateur investors were attracted by the prospect of a quick and certain gain on a market which seemed to be forever rising. Stockbrokers were allowing people to buy on margin, that is, not paying the full price but hoping to get their money back when the investor sold their shares. Brokers in turn were financing their positions by borrowing from banks. The debts of brokers piled up. The London stock market was also on a bull run. This came to an end in September 1929 when a group of prominent investors led by Clarence Hatry were convicted of fraud. The London market crashed. Nervousness spread across the Atlantic. In New York, on October 24, 1929, known as Black Thursday, the Dow Jones stock market index fell by 11 percent. Following desperate attempts by "market leaders" to calm matters, the market experienced a second and then a third fall within days, dropping by 13 percent and then a further 12 percent. Brokers were bankrupted, as were the banks who had lent them money. Assets worth millions were now worth thousands. Everyone was selling to retrieve the little that was left. This was a catastrophic turn of events. The Dow Jones did not return to its September 1929 peak till 25 years later, in 1954.

The downward spiral that followed was called the Great Depression and lasted from 1929 till 1941 in the US – the dates for European countries vary depending on individual country circumstances. In the US in 1929, GDP in nominal terms was $103.6 million ($976.1 million in 2005 dollar terms) and it did not exceed that level till 1941, when it was $126.7 million ($1,365.0 million in 2005 dollars). In the UK, the period before the Depression was one of stagnation so when the Depression came it was just another dip. But after a political crisis which led to the breakup of the Labour Party and the exit of the UK from the Gold Standard in 1931, things began to bottom out. The Depression in the UK lasted for five years, from 1929 to 1934. But in the US the situation was more serious and unemployment reached the unprecedented level of 25 percent. Unable to repay their mortgage debts, many farmers lost their farms and had to migrate in large numbers from the Midwest to the West Coast or the big cities. The tumultuous and harrowing impact that the Great Depression had on the lives of the farming community was immortalized in John Steinbeck's moving novel *The Grapes of Wrath*. In some sense, the US had caught up with Europe in the misery caused by the collapse of the Old Economy. The Federal Reserve, the American equivalent of the Bank of England, believed that the boom had overextended itself due to cheap money and began to restrict the supply of money and credit. Many American banks failed as prices of goods and assets collapsed. Loans they had given out were not repaid.

The preeminent economists of the day, ever faithful to the orthodox doctrine, believed that the solution to the crisis resided in the market. Their theories did not need any correction. What was needed was more austerity, more severe wage cuts and higher interest rates. The idea was that the economy would only move back to the old equilibrium level if governments stopped interfering and let the markets work. It was left to the younger generation of economists to question this orthodoxy and search for alternatives. It was not easy. The first attempts made did not quite solve the problems but they did leave a legacy that has endured. Three economists – Keynes in Britain, Myrdal in Sweden, and Hayek, originally from Vienna but later settled in Britain – made brave attempts to update Wicksell's ideas on the workings of a monetary economy. Since these were false starts we need not dwell on them too much but it is worth recounting them because their ideas have not gone away.

The False Dawn

John Maynard Keynes was the senior among the three. He had already acquired a reputation as a brilliant controversialist, having denounced the postwar settlement of Versailles as disastrous for Germany and publicly criticized the British establishment for the return to gold at the wrong parity. He was an active player in the stock market, a prolific writer of articles for periodicals and taught economics as a Fellow of King's College, Cambridge.

Keynes's two-volume work *The Treatise on Money* was untypical of the man as he was not a writer of comprehensive tomes on a topic. He himself regarded the work as a failure. But he was trying to relate the monetary side of the economy to the

real side by looking at how price level reacts to excess demand –
what happens when investments exceed savings, how profits can
be a disequilibrium phenomenon which drives a boom forward,
and the mechanics behind how financial flows in and out of the
industrial and commercial sector and back into the purely speculative financial sector happen and their impact on the course of
the economy. As he wrote in the preface to the *Treatise*, his objective was "to find a method which is useful in describing, not
merely the characteristics of static equilibrium, but also those of
disequilibrium and to discover the dynamical laws governing
the passage of a monetary system from one position of equilibrium to another."

This was an ambitious program and had he achieved it,
economics might have charted a different path. But *The Treatise
on Money* lacked a clear model that could be used to understand
the economy when in equilibrium and disequilibrium. Despite
its ambition, the work failed to gain the attention Keynes had
hoped for it.

Keynes's contemporary, Friedrich Hayek (1899–1992), was a
brilliant free market economist. Trained in Vienna, he was steeped
in the orthodoxy of Walrasian economics but also aware of
Wicksell's work. Along with Gunnar Myrdal (1898–1987), a
socialist, who succeeded Gustav Cassel as professor at the
University of Stockholm, he proposed an alternative approach.
Later, Hayek and Myrdal, whose politics were poles apart, were to
share the Nobel Prize in Economics in 1974 for "their pioneering
work in the theory of money and economic fluctuations."

Hayek and Myrdal took Wicksell's idea of the gap between the natural rate and the market rate as their starting point. Hayek, in his lauded publication *Prices and Production*, based on a series of lectures given at the LSE in 1931, argued that the explanation for the Depression lay in banks lending money at low interest rates to prospective investors. Low rates made those projects feasible which had a distant payoff. These projects would enhance the productivity of the economy (somewhat like Schumpeter's innovations, though Hayek did not use that analogy). But the economy was by assumption at full capacity, producing goods with old technology which had a shorter payoff. The new investors diverted inputs from the old technology to their new long-term projects. These inputs were harnessed to produce more output than before but at a point in the distant future. Meanwhile the old technology's output was reduced as it was starved of inputs.

A simplistic, but unrealistic analogy, would be to think of an economy producing just one consumption good – hamburgers. Someone invents a way of producing leaner hamburgers by raising better cattle but these cattle will take time to produce lean beef. The old hamburger technology loses resources – inputs – to the new project. Output of hamburgers goes down while waiting for the leaner cattle to yield beef and consequently the price of hamburgers goes up as their supply is curtailed.

The diversion of inputs without a matching output of consumables causes inflation, and credit has to expand to keep pace with rising costs. Sooner rather than later, the banks panic;

stopping any further credit and hiking up the interest rate. This leads to the projects with a long-run payoff – in this case the cattle yielding leaner beef – being abandoned, incomplete and with idle but unusable intermediate inputs and idle labor. It takes a long time for the older businesses to reabsorb the idle inputs and hence the recession is prolonged. The low interest rate has distorted the "price gradient" between short- and long-run goods and until that is restored there will be no return to full employment.

Hayek's construction of his argument was vitiated by his reliance on the Austrian capital theory, which proved an obstacle for most of his readers. But the idea that cheap credit causes unsustainable booms by encouraging "mal-investments" was well taken and has a contemporary resonance. He also took the view that the recovery would take a long time before the economy returned to the "normalcy" which prevailed before the boom began. Hayek had no policy nostrums; his only recommendation was patience while waiting for the market to work the poison of previous mal-investments out of the system.

Ironically, Myrdal's *Monetary Equilibrium* was a sharp critique of Wicksell, pointing out that Wicksell's equilibrium condition – that the natural rate and the market rate should be equal – was valid only for a static economy. In a dynamic economy, the rates of return that equilibrate savings and investment crucially depend upon expectations. Myrdal distinguished between *ex ante* calculations of rates of return, which were made under uncertainty, and *ex post*, when one could be sure of what had happened.

Entrepreneurs invest on the basis of an expected or *ex ante* rate of return; what they realize is the actual or *ex post* rate of return. The gap between the two drives the economy. Myrdal made the radical suggestion that Wicksell's notion of price stability as the *sine qua non* of a monetary equilibrium was inapplicable to a dynamic economy. In such an economy, inventions constantly improved productivity and raised the natural rate of interest. This meant that the task of the banking system was constantly to adjust the market rate to keep up with it. Prices should be falling if productivity was going up and not remain stable. Prices could fluctuate but the important thing was to allow the process of innovation and productivity growth to proceed.

While neither Hayek nor Myrdal had any immediate policy impact, their ideas proved fruitful in the long run.

A New Toolbox for Economists

Ever since they began, statistics – records of trade and money flows, prices and shipments – have been an integral part of economics. Gregory King (1648–1712), a confidential advisor to the British government, was a pioneer in "political arithmetic," a statistical stocktaking of the resources of the nation in order to, among other things, gauge its ability to fight wars. Malthus continued this tradition in his extensive research into population and food statistics across the world in the second and subsequent editions of his *Essay on Population*. But it was not until after World War I that a new discipline – econometrics – took shape.

Econometrics, founded on the intersection between math and statistical methods, allows economists to attach numbers to the various forces and tendencies in economic life. How much is the demand for a commodity or service sensitive to changes in its price; what, in other words, is its price elasticity? How much excess money can an economy accommodate before the rate of price rises – inflation – reaches 5 percent per annum or 10 percent? Mathematics enables economists to formulate these questions in terms of simple equations with variables (known quantities) and parameters (unknown influences to be measured). With the data for the variables, the parameters of the equations can be estimated (though never truly known). Statistical methods exist to attach degrees of confidence to the estimates.

It all began with a stockbroker Alfred Cowles asking his statistician friend Henry Moore, a Professor of Statistics, if one could perform a correlation among 22 variables. Moore was uncertain as to why anyone would want to do so, but said yes, it could be done. Cowles wanted to relate the variables to the movement of stock prices. He found these calculations useful enough to endow a foundation – the Cowles Foundation (later Cowles Commission) – to encourage research in econometrics. The Econometric Society was founded in 1933 as an international society of scholars interested in using econometrics to understand economies better.

Over the past 80 years, computer technology has evolved substantially from the mechanically operated analog computers to the miniature digital laptops that we have today. Economic data have also proliferated so that we have numbers on every aspect of the economy and across many economies. Data are also available at higher frequencies – not just annual or quarterly but in the case of stock prices minute by minute. They can be downloaded on to computers and calculations can be carried out for parameters of equations, which in turn may drive buy or sell activities. Econometric models are available for national economies, for commodities, for companies, and much more. They begin with a mathematical formulation of the economic relationship. Most often a linear form is chosen. Thus if we want to explain the amount demanded for a commodity we call it y and its price, which would be an explanatory variable, x. The resulting linear equation would be $y = a - bx$ while a nonlinear one would be $y = a + b (1/x)$ (x to the power of –1), to give simple examples. The statistical part then comes in whereby the relationship is taken to be not exact but probabilistic. To convey this a random (or stochastic) error (or shock) term is added to the equation ($y = a - bx + u$). This is to allow for the basic uncertainty of all economic events, as well as to allow for many other variables which have to be omitted to keep the relationship simple. If the basic equation is sound, then it will explain a large part of the variation in the variable we are interested in, in our case y, the amount bought of a commodity. A measure of the "goodness of fit" is the correlation coefficient r or its square R^2 (R squared). Many equations together constitute a model and there are more sophisticated measures of the explanatory powers of a model. The use of econometric techniques is widespread now in public and private sector decision-making. Increasingly numbers have become an indispensable part of the toolkit of economists. The Econometric Society was born at a time when economics itself was about to become more mathematically oriented and would require the services of experts who could translate policy advice into specific numbers. The fruits of such technical ways of studying economies were not long in coming.

The Riddle of Income Growth

One of the early fruits of econometrics was to provide an answer to the contentious question of whether the Industrial Revolution had improved the economic conditions of workers. A debate had raged among British economic historians, politically divided as they were between the Marxist left and the traditional right. The means to finding a definitive answer were to come from the US.

Paul Douglas (1892–1976), who taught at the University of Chicago and became a senator in his later life, worked at gathering data on wages and prices to obtain a series on real wages for the US economy. He and a colleague, Charles Cobb, proposed a mathematical function which became known as the Cobb-Douglas Production Function.[6] The idea was to express output as determined by two input variables – capital and labor. The two "factors of production," as they were labeled, combined multiplicatively but with different exponents (weights). Using annual data on national income, employment and a measure of capital stock, they could estimate the exponents. Doing this, they arrived at some startling conclusions. The first was that the shares of labor and capital in total income were constant over the 50-odd years of data Douglas had collected. Unlike in Great Britain, US workers had not suffered a flattening of wage growth. What was more exciting was that the algebraic form enabled them to show that the exponent attached to each factor matched its share in total income and also that, if as neoclassical theory posited workers were paid a real wage equal to their marginal product and similarly for capital, the outcome would be the constant shares explained by their function.

Thus we were in the best of all possible worlds. As economic growth took place, the productivity of labor rose. But this was rewarded by higher real wages. The resulting constancy of shares was something of a statistical miracle but seemed to confirm an optimistic view of capitalism that the Americans, unlike the Europeans, had always had. What was more, the results bolstered neoclassical microeconomic theory. The exponents, when estimated, also summed to one (hence the shares added up to one) and this also indicated that for the economy as a whole, there were constant returns to scale, that is, if you doubled both inputs, output would also double.

The idea that the share of wages would be a constant fraction of total national income proved to be very powerful in the interwar period. In an appendix to his *General Theory*, Keynes called it "one of the most surprising, yet best established facts in the whole range of economic statistics, both for the Great Britain and for the United States." He cites tables in which the share in Great Britain from 1924 to 1935 comes out between 41 percent and 44 percent, while for USA for 1919 to 1934 it is between 34 percent and 37 percent.

As we shall see later, few things stay constant in the realm of economics. The trend and cycles in the share of wages turn out to be one of the keys to understanding the Great Recession.

Riding the Waves with Eugen Slutsky

If you plot the course of income or sales or investment, it will look like a wave. The literature on business cycles often uses the term long waves to describe the data. There are often systematic reasons why there are cycles. Indeed, as we've seen, Marx, Wicksell and Schumpeter among others looked for explanations of the cycles. At Columbia University in the immediate aftermath of World War I, Wesley Clair Mitchell (1874–1948) launched an extensive program of measuring business cycles. He chose a variety of time series – rail shipments, bank loans, agricultural output and prices, sales and inventories, etc. For each variable, he wanted to locate the trough and the peak and then measure the length of the cycle from peak to peak or trough to trough. The exercise was conducted without any prior theory informing the statistical work. The task was to gather the data first and then seek an explanation. Mitchell, with his co-author Arthur Burns, concluded after a lifetime of research that business cycles in the US were on average around 3.5 years in length, but with a lot dispersion around the average. These were therefore short cycles.

Mitchell's research was independently validated by the work of Joseph Kitchin (1861–1932).[7] In 1923, Kitchin published his study of cycles in American and British data for 1890–1922. He found short cycles of 40 months and major cycles of between 7 and 11 years. Kitchin thus also corroborates the ten-year cycle of Juglar and Marx.

Other economists such as Simon Kuznets, a Nobel Laureate, and Moses Abramovitz as well as W. Arthur Lewis, another Nobel Prize winner, discovered longer cycles of between 14 and 22 years in length. Cycles could be thus discerned in the data. But an explanation for what caused cycles remained elusive: Was it investment in house-building, or demographics? The long gestation period required for large-scale investment in steel and shipbuilding? Or the fluctuating sentiments of consumers?

There is, however, the occurrence of chance events. I may have the money to buy something but I may postpone the purchase. Many people may have the same idea if my postponement has to do with adverse weather – snowfall, for example. These "random" occurrences often shift the data up or down, overlaying the systematic influences of price or interest rates or income. It was a Russian economist and statistician Eugen Slutsky (1880–1948), a middle-aged Russian professor who was virtually unknown to economists in the US and Europe, who conjectured that if you have many such separate random events, their sum may exhibit a wave-like pattern. Thus without any systematic influences, random events alone if summed together would give the impression of a cyclical wave.

To prove this Slutsky conducted a bold experiment. Taking a selection of winning numbers from the Soviet lottery, he summed them up to obtain three random series. Subjecting these to statistical techniques similar to those of time series, he plotted these against English business cycle data for 1855–77; the similarity was striking. Slutsky's experiment showed that shocks that had been generated by random events, but were not themselves cyclical, could create oscillations in economic variables.[8] This raised a perennial problem in statistical reasoning. Does the similarity say that all cycles are caused by random events or just that similar shapes are possible but not informative?

One way in which such random events, or "shocks" as they are often called, can sum up is if each shock has effects which linger beyond the initial effect. Thus, if the snowfall delays purchases this weekend, the next weekend may lead to extra purchases. This would be a negative "auto" correlation across the two weeks of the accidental element in purchases. Or the snowfall may persist and the purchases may be delayed for longer, week after week. That would be a positive auto-correlation. What may then occur is that the first and later effects of one shock – snowfall – may overlap with the effects of another shock – say a royal wedding, which excites spending – and together they may start a wave.

The Rocking Horse of Ragnar Frisch

It was a young Norwegian economist Ragnar Frisch (1895–1973) who in 1933 made a profound contribution to our understanding of the nature of cycles. Thirty-five years later, Frisch was to share the first Nobel Prize in Economics with his fellow econometrician the Dutch Professor Jan Tinbergen. Frisch compared the economy to a rocking horse. The horse would be stationary if left alone. But if touched, it would start rocking back and forth. Soon, however, the movements would cease and the horse would revert to its stationary mode. The rocking horse is so designed that it can be at rest or it can rock back and forth if pushed. It needs an external "shock" to start the movements. But if you were to witness movements persisting, it could only mean that shocks were being given to the rocking horse (and by analogy the economy) repeatedly. These shocks need not come at regular or predictable intervals, but without repeated shocks there would be no cycles.[9]

The Walrasian economic model could thus be seen as a picture of the rocking horse at rest – static or stationary. But since cycles were endemic in capitalist economies, there must be repeated shocks. This simple hypothesis proved very powerful. Econometric methods modeled data on the basis of probability laws. The best explanation of any economic phenomenon – income, prices, demand, supply – would leave an unexplained residual. This would be the unexplained, unexplainable random part of the behavior of economic data. This random part is similar to a shock; it occurs but in unpredictable ways. The idea of a stable economy subjected to shocks became a staple of business cycle theorizing once Frisch had introduced the idea.

This process of overlapping shocks, along with their delayed effects, adds a dimension to Frisch's rocking horse hypothesis. One can see why this idea would combine with Slutsky's theory to provide a fuller explanation of the economy's cyclical behavior. Thus the shocks given to the rocking horse may be random. But if they have delayed effects and overlap with one another, you may observe a cyclical pattern in the data over and above the systematic effects of income, interest rates, etc. Econometrics was to prove a very useful tool in studying such issues, both at a theoretical level and then in estimating equations of models which were designed to predict the course of the economy.

The world needed an answer to get it out of its misery during the Great Depression. The answer came from Keynes.

PART TWO

Chapter Four

CAUSING A STIR

John Maynard Keynes was not like other economists. He did not stay in his ivory tower and pen articles and books. He was a man of affairs – speculator in the stock market, chairman of an insurance company, journalist, author of a bestseller, civil servant during the war and after, controversialist, patron of the arts, friend of authors and painters, husband of a ballerina, and a Fellow of King's College, Cambridge who also looked after its finances. He was ever aware of the need to use his supercharged brain to tackle urgent problems of the day. He wrote in newspapers and weeklies, published pamphlets, gave evidence before expert committees, coached his friends in the Liberal Party in economic policy-making, preached, proselytized and proclaimed nostrums for relieving problems as he saw fit.

In these matters he was very much like David Ricardo. Early on in the Great Depression, he saw that everything he had thought of as economic theory, including his own two-volume *Treatise on Money*, was useless for solving the deep crisis at hand. So he began all over again, constructing a new answer. He had his acolytes, young economists Richard Kahn, Joan Robinson, James Meade, Piero Sraffa – all Fellows of Cambridge colleges and many his former students – his "Circus," as he called them. He used his Circus as a sounding board and they responded with their criticisms and suggestions.[1]

The Keynesian Revolution

Keynes's protégé Richard Kahn, like him a Fellow of King's College, had planted the germ of a revolutionary idea in an article Keynes had published in the *Economic Journal*, a prestigious journal of which he was the editor. The idea was simple. Any money spent by the government on projects that employed workers – such as building roads – would return in a multiple of the original sum. This was because workers, hard up as they always are, would spend most of their wages buying things for consumption. This would mean that items sold by the shopkeepers would need to be restocked, which would in turn pay the wages of workers in factories making them. The money would circulate. At each round most of it would be spent and the spiral would mount. Kahn was able to give a formula for how much the initial money would multiply by. If the workers typically consumed four-fifths of their wage (80 percent) then the final sum of all the rounds of spending would be five times the initial amount. Or, in other words, the reciprocal of one less the initial spending proportion: $1/(1 - 0.8) = 1/0.2 = 5$. This was the multiplier.

This insight made a revolutionary impact. Government spending had up until this point been thought of as wasteful. Mr. Gladstone, Britain's famous nineteenth-century Prime Minister and Chancellor of the Exchequer, wished to leave money in the pockets of people to fructify. Here was an idea which said that money fructified not by staying in the pockets of the taxpayers but by being spent on projects which employed people. Further paradoxes followed. If a government were to save, that is, cut spending in a depression, it would worsen the problem because private spending would shrink even more as employment declined. Individual households benefited by saving. But if all households saved, they would end up poorer as a lack of demand for goods would mean that fewer workers were required. This was the "fallacy of aggregation."

Savings would fructify if there was investment to match them. That was the old doctrine. But investors would look to future profits. If the economy was depressed, why would they invest when it might result in a loss? In a depression, investment was needed regardless of profit expectations. Only the government could do this. That would be enough to get the economy moving again if the multiplier process of Richard Kahn operated.

It was left to Keynes to sew together the insights on the multiplier into a general theory of how total income or employment was determined in a modern industrialized economy. He had to add a theory of investment and a theory of interest. *The General Theory of Employment, Interest and Money* was hailed as a revolution in economics – the Keynesian Revolution.

The urgent problem of the time was to understand why market economies were susceptible to large-scale unemployment. It was not unknown for people to be unemployed but this was thought to be a personal tragedy or a temporary glitch in the way markets worked. But here was unemployment which was widespread and persistent. It was an underemployment equilibrium. Such a situation was not thought possible, as Ricardo had argued with Malthus a century and more previously.

Keynes showed that underemployment equilibria were not only possible but, if steps were not taken to counter them, they could be endemic to a free market system. To convince his fellow economists (to whom he said his book was addressed) he introduced some new vocabulary, words redolent of the psychology so fashionable in the 1930s thanks to Sigmund Freud's popularity – concepts such as the propensity to consume, liquidity preference, and the exotic notion of animal spirits. He proposed public investment as a solution when private investment was too shy to undertake new enterprise. His ideas were taken up by governments and they shaped budgets, the language of economic policy, and the contents of textbooks.

But over the years the model has been challenged by economists who still adhere to the theories of Ricardo–Walras–Marshall. They say that Keynes's argument about involuntary unemployment depends crucially on the assumption of a rigid money wage. They reject his theory of the interest rate (see below) by arguing that "real" factors of saving and investment are more important than liquidity preference. There is a similar disagreement about the toolkit that Keynes bequeathed to the world. They question the efficacy of running a deficit to boost income and employment, arguing that this will undermine confidence and "crowd out" private investment. They oppose monetary stimulus, predicting it will have an inflationary consequence.

Today, Keynesian economics is an embattled subject rather than a triumphant revolution. Within 50 years of its publication in 1936, the message of the *General Theory* was being disputed, if not discarded. In this part of the book I want to take you through this difficult terrain.

The Model

In creating his new approach, Keynes tried to use ideas with which economists of his day were familiar. Aware that his first and most important task would be to convince his fellow economists of the validity of what he was putting forward, he addressed them directly in the preface to the *General Theory* and stated that the work itself was "a long struggle of escape . . . from habitual modes of thought and expression."

A new generation of economists responded eagerly. The misery caused by the Great Depression had stirred an awareness of the crucial role that economic policy could and should play in alleviating human suffering. It was no longer satisfying to hear the older generation of economists say "Leave it to the market." Activism was the answer and Keynes's analysis offered the tools. Soon after the book was published came the outbreak of World War II, and the crucial role that the government played in resource mobilization and harnessing the fruits of research and development to the war effort provided further support to the case for state intervention. Keynesian ideas became the dominant paradigm in the teaching of economics. The students who came to study economics, many born during the Depression and others returning from the war to pursue further studies, some taking advantage of America's GI Bill, were ripe for the new message. This was for them "the new economics," as Seymour Harris, a Harvard professor, called Keynesian theory. Even so, the older generation did not accept the ideas readily. From the outset, there was a questioning of Keynes's theory. Resistance to Keynes's ideas began as early as its popular acceptance. The criticism can be divided into two strands. One was rejection and the other was a crippling (some would say a fatal) embrace.

Keynes's Argument

Unemployment was a fact, but it was taken to be a temporary, transient phenomenon by the rejectionists and one that had a simple solution – cut wages. Keynes's proposition that it could be an *equilibrium* – a systematic outcome and one from which a move away is difficult – shook the older generation of economists. It implied that workers willing to take on a job at the prevailing wage would not be able to get jobs. The standard explanation of unemployment had been that workers were pricing themselves out of the market by demanding work at a higher wage than was available. The solution in that case was for them to accept a cut in the wage level. According to the theory stemming from Walras and Marshall, if there was excess supply, a reduction in price would restore equilibrium between demand and supply. This was as true of the labor market as it was of the market for bananas.

But the relevant price to be cut, according to the theory, was the real wage level. Keynes argued that in a monetary economy, that is in real life, workers and employers negotiated in terms of the money wage. How could a worker offer to cut his real wage? At best, he could accept a lower money wage. Whether the real wage went down as a result would depend on what happened to the relevant prices, principally of the goods workers bought for consumption. These would be decided by the producers, not the workers; and not by the individual employers who were bargaining with the workers but all the producers in aggregate. If prices were to fall *along* with wages then a cut in money wages would not lead to an equal fall in real wages. So, according to Keynes, this road to restoring employment would not work. In reality, real wages rose during the Great Depression while there was a lot of unemployment.

Having closed off one neoclassical route for restoring full employment, Keynes proceeded to argue that total employment was determined by aggregate effective demand rather than real wages. Aggregate *effective* demand was the amount of spending that would result from the decisions of consumers to purchase goods depending on their income, and the decisions of producers to invest in their businesses by buying additional machinery or building factories. The sum of the consumer spending and investment would be the aggregate demand price. The producers would plan to produce and hire labor depending on their expectations of the revenues they would get from selling their output. This was the economy's aggregate supply price.

Keynes very much wanted to persuade his fellow economists of the novelty of his ideas, but he wanted to soften the shock of the new by using familiar terms. Hence, he used the labels supply and demand for his new concepts, albeit adding "aggregate" as an adjective. Yet his use of the word price to describe total revenue or total proceeds was confusing. He thought that the demand and supply curves at the aggregate level would have the same familiarity as the Marshallian demand and supply curves.

But he muddled matters further along the way by plotting his price (total revenue) not against the quantity of output, as in Marshall, but against employment. He did this because he felt that at the aggregate level the idea of total output did not make much sense since the composition of total output was heterogeneous – adding apples and pears to bread and bicycles. (Nowadays we do it all the time when we use the notion of GNP or GDP.) He presumed that he could make the total employment level more homogeneous by taking the aggregate wage bill and dividing it by a basic money wage – a wage unit. Simply put, the method would treat a worker earning twice the wage unit as two workers. This way he had defined employment in terms of "wage units."

The aggregate supply curve sloped from the bottom left upward to the right, telling us that as more workers were employed the costs of production would mount disproportionately as diminishing returns set in (see Figure 2). This was pretty much standard theory. Keynes's innovation was that the aggregate demand curve rose sharply from the lower left and then

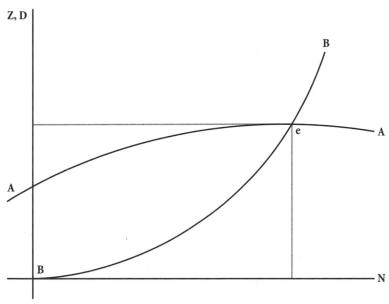

Z, D Total revenues and total costs expected
N Employment in wage units

Figure 2 Keynes's aggregate demand (AA) and aggregate supply (BB) curves

leveled off after a while. This was because of his idea of the consumption function. This related consumption to income, but argued that as income rose consumption would rise less than proportionately. You could think of this either as saying that at lower incomes people spend their entire income on their daily needs but at higher incomes there is scope for saving. Or, you could posit that as a family's income increases, it will spend a smaller proportion of its additional income. The marginal propensity to consume (MPC) – the ratio of additional consumption to additional income – was less than one.

The intersection of the two curves – aggregate demand and aggregate supply – determined total employment. Keynes's argument was that this level of employment might fall short of full employment; there might be workers willing to work who would not find employment. They were *involuntarily* unemployed. Aggregate demand was inadequate to ensure full employment. But if aggregate demand fell short of the full employment level, how could demand be raised to the level at which full employment would result? Consumption was determined by income and largely workers' income. Income could only rise if there was an increase in employment but employment itself would only rise if incomes rose. Thus there is circularity in relying on consumption to raise employment.

The second large component of aggregate effective demand was investment spending by entrepreneurs. Investment could be used to increase employment. But how could investment be increased? And what determined the level of investment? Keynes's theory of investment argued that any proposed expenditure on real investment would generate an expected income stream stretching into the future. There would be a variety of rates of discount which could be applied to this stream of future income. The rate of discount at which the future income stream would equal the amount invested was the marginal efficiency of capital (MEC). As long as the MEC was above the interest rate prevailing in the market, investment could occur and even increase.

Investment is, however, a future-oriented activity, unlike consumption. It is a gamble that the calculation of expected profits will turn out to be correct. The world is full of uncertainty which is difficult to insure against. In the end, it is the animal spirits of the investors which, for Keynes, is the determining variable rather than costs or returns. The idea of animal spirits is appealing but imprecise. Keynes's theory of investment is in all respects quite conventional. The addition of the idea of animal spirits makes it look exotic but it is not clear how animal spirits actually make a difference. Keynes distinguished between risk and uncertainty. Risk was something which could be calculated in a similar way to computing the probability of throwing seven in a throw of two dice; uncertainty could not be calculated in the same way. It was radically incalculable. Animal spirits, an intuitive gut feeling, was a way entrepreneurs had of coping with uncertainty. As animal spirits swung between lion-like and mouse-like, investment fluctuated. But besides mentioning the words animal spirits, Keynes did not elaborate on the concept much.

Shorn of animal spirits, Keynes's theory of investment turns out to be quite conventional – comparing likely return and the rate of interest. But he was keen to downplay the role of interest rates. The rate of interest, he argued, would have a very limited effect on the decision to invest, even if the monetary authorities could cut the rate. But there were limits to how much the rate of interest could be cut.

The logic behind why the rate of interest could not be cut was another of Keynes's innovations. He argued that, unlike in classical theory, or even in Wicksell, where interest rate equilibrated real savings and real investment, as it were in a barter economy, interest rate was a purely monetary phenomenon and would be determined by the interaction of the demand for money and the supply of money. The supply of money was under the control of the Central Bank or the monetary authorities. The demand for money was motivated by three impulses, much as Marshall had suggested. First was the transactions motive – have money ready to buy things. Second was the precautionary motive – have some for a rainy day. The third motive was speculative – to grab the bargain you see in the shops or, in the case of people who traded money for securities, in the hope of making a profit based on the up and down movement in the price of the securities. The first two motives were passive and predictable. They were stable parts of the demand for money. It was the last, the speculative motive, which determined the level of the interest rate. Keynes used a psychological expression when labeling the demand for money as liquidity preference.

The speculative motive is, of course, the most active among the three motives for holding money. To explain this, Keynes concentrated on just one type of security – the consol. This is a bond with a fixed rate of interest (coupon) but no maturity date. The price of the bond goes above or below par as the actual rate in the market goes above or below the coupon rate on the consol. Thus if you possess a £100 consol with a £5 coupon and the actual rate goes down to 4 percent, the demand for your consol will rise until its price is £125 so that the £5 coupon is just a 4 percent rate of return.

Thus the price of the bond is inversely related to the rate of interest. This is the *long-run rate of interest* which is of relevance to the investment decision. Monetary authorities operate on the short-run rate of interest by dealing with banks and releasing or withholding reserves. Alternatively they could signal to banks to ease their lending to borrowers, especially those likely to be in the bond market. The hope would be that by expanding the money supply and lowering the short-run rate, some people in the bond market would be encouraged to buy bonds and thus the long-run rate will fall.

At any moment, there would be some investors expecting the bond price to go down (the long-run interest rate to go up) and those expecting the bond price to go up (the interest rate to go down). Normally the market would be divided between the two types and they would buy and sell the bonds to each other. The more a rate goes down, the fewer people would expect it go down further and more would expect a rise. But if the rate had gone down so much that most people expected the next move to be up, then investors would not buy the bonds, since it might lead to a loss as the bond price fell. As Keynes wrote, "the rate of interest is a highly conventional, rather than a highly psychological, phenomenon. For its actual value is largely governed by the prevailing view as to what its value is expected to be."[2]

The monetary authorities might try to pump more money into the system but people would prefer to leave the money idle, earning zero interest, than exchange it for bonds. There was a *liquidity trap* where the rate of interest reached a floor, and no further fall could be engineered by the monetary authorities. Recent policies of quantitative easing have seen Central Banks buying bonds and other assets on the open market to lower the rate of interest, both short term and long run. The short rate has reached a floor of below 0.5 percent and that is what a liquidity trap looks like.

The novelty of terms such as consumption function and the marginal propensity to consume attracted the younger generation of economists. These terms looked more scientific and in tune with the then fashionable psychology. The system was amenable to mathematical treatment. During the war, scientific research into new weapons had been harnessed by both sides. Natural science had glamour for the young. Now economics was taking on a much more scientific look with a new theory which promised to deal with problems of unemployment in the same way that science had helped win the war. But the real coup was that with these concepts Keynes could justify an increase in public spending as self-financing. Since neither consumer spending nor investment could be expected to increase endogenously – by itself or by market activity – the only way to raise the level of employment would be to rely on a force which did not depend on market behavior. It had to be autonomous. This was government spending.

The prevailing orthodoxy was one that favored balanced budgets and regarded public spending as a waste of resources. The money that had been taxed from the private sector to fund public spending could be put to more productive use by the private sector. Using an expression developed later, public spending would "crowd out" private spending, and thus delay the automatic forces of recovery. But the problem was that during the Depression, neither the workers nor business people were spending much money. To revive the economy, the government could begin by spending some money – say on road-building or ditch-digging programs. The multiplier would then move into action.

The economists who enthusiastically adopted Keynes's theory did not much like the marginal efficiency of capital as a concept and replaced the investment relationship by the accelerator principle, a formulation first proposed by an American economist, J. M. Clark. The idea was that business people added to their capital stock if they had experienced or expected a rise in their sales. At the aggregate level, this was translated into change in GDP, actual or expected. As a consequence, the role of interest rates was completely downgraded. The Keynesian model was simplified to a multiplier-accelerator model by Paul Samuelson, the first economist to so christen the model when he explored the possibility of cycles using Keynesian logic.[3] As to Keynes's monetary theory, followers concluded that monetary policy would be ineffective as a tool for recovery. They also took seriously Keynes's idea that in the long run it would be necessary to drive the interest rate to zero. Keynes was worried that rich societies would suffer from excess savings, which would act as a barrier to high demand and hence prevent full employment. Fiscal policy was the sole driving force for full employment.

There began to appear an American version of Keynesianism, as against a British or rather a Cambridge (UK) version. British economists considered the American version a distorted version of Keynesianism; "Bastard Keynesianism," as Joan Robinson called it. This was because it was simplified somewhat and apt to be less critical of the private economy than British adherents liked. For Americans, Keynesian policies were simply a top-up, to be used to keep an otherwise healthy and dynamic economy from falling into recessions. The American economy was growing rapidly through the postwar years except for two short recessions in 1949 and 1957. The British economy had been damaged in the war and had a severe shortage of capital stock. Its growth was constrained by the balance of trade problem. If exports did not keep up with imports, there would be a deficit in the balance of trade and money could move out, putting pressure on the pound sterling. Then the economy would have to be slowed down, raising unemployment. But unemployment was politically unpopular so soon reflation would be introduced. This was the Stop-Go cycle. The need was for better control of the private spending in the economy. For British economists, Keynesianism was a critique of a private enterprise economy's endemic failure to guarantee full employment. It proposed much-needed radical changes to the economy as well as to policy. British economists were much more likely to advocate income redistribution as a way of guaranteeing full employment than their American counterparts. American economists were also more likely to suggest tax cuts rather than spending increases. The British were advocates of high tax as well as high budget deficits.

Keynes was not advocating endless deficits or a disregard for public debt. Indeed the logic of the multiplier is that the initial spending will generate enough extra income so that the spending will be self-liquidating by means of extra tax revenue generated. For an economy where resources are idle, the reactivation of these resources is a powerful justification for spending the money initially, even if it raises a deficit in the short term.

Keynes genuinely meant his work to be a general theory for the economy which would be applicable whether there was involuntary unemployment or full employment. He also tentatively hinted that a monetary economy such as one lives in everyday should be theorized in a different way than the logic of barter that the Ricardo–Walras–Marshall schemes required. But his persuasive policy solution for the immediate crisis was so powerful that economists did not bother with his larger purpose. Keynes's theory was reduced down to the idea that government spending can work to raise output and employment in a depressed economy.

Rejectionists Fight Back

The rejectionists remained unconvinced. They looked for a chink in Keynes's armor. Here they were helped by another slight muddle Keynes himself created. He had assumed the money wage to be given for the initial exposition of his argument. He had also used the money wage unit to reduce all types of labor to a homogeneous number. Keynes's use of the wage unit was not taken up by his followers. But his detractors used this to undermine Keynes's conclusion, arguing that his theory of involuntary unemployment in a free market was based on the assumption of a rigid money wage. If the money wage was flexible, then there could be no underemployment equilibrium; if there is unemployment then it has to be temporary while we wait for the wage to come down. The money wage was rigid because of trade unions. Since the mood of the times was in favor of trade unions, this was taken as a plausible rigidity that could not be easily eliminated. In later years, the idea that Keynes's theory required a rigid money wage became an accepted argument even among his followers and was to cause much damage to the cogency of his message.

Another strand of attack was led by Pigou, Keynes's teacher and his colleague at King's College. In the *General Theory*, while criticizing classical economics, Keynes had used Pigou's writings as a typical example of the fallacies prevalent. Pigou was made a whipping boy by Keynes. However, Pigou came back with a fundamental objection to Keynes's theory which struck home. In 1943, in an article in the *Economic Journal* entitled "The

Classical Stationary State," Pigou pointed out that while Keynes had explained why wages or interest rates were not likely to be the instruments to restore full employment, he had neglected an important area.[4] As Keynes had accepted, people held money in liquid form, either as cash or as bank deposits. These were their money balances. As a depression proceeded, prices would come down. The money balances held by consumers would effectively be worth more in terms of purchasing power. Their *real balances* would increase. In such circumstances, consumers might be more willing to spend from their money balances in spite of their depressed incomes. Thus spending out of money balances provides a market-based route for restoring full employment. There would be no need to resort to public spending. This particular strand was termed the real balance effect, or the Pigou effect, and provided an effective counterattack against Keynesian domination in economics.

The Crippling Embrace

John Hicks (1904–89) had been at Cambridge while Keynes was writing his *General Theory*. Yet Hicks was not part of the Circus. He was an associate of Dennis Robertson (1890–1963), who was thought to be in Pigou's camp. Cambridge economics was then, and continued to be later on, a very divided world. Hicks was not privy to any of the discussions that had gone into the writing of the *General Theory*. Yet he had the most profound influence of anyone on how Keynes's message was received.

Hicks translated the core content of the *General Theory* into the more familiar form of the Marshallian Cross and brought out the general equilibrium aspects of Keynes's theory. He did this in a short article entitled "Mr Keynes and the 'Classics': A Suggested Interpretation," which appeared in *Econometrica*, the recently founded journal of the Econometric Society, in 1937.[5] Hicks's IS-LM diagram (IS-LL in the original article) threw the exotic parts of Keynes's model away – including the aggregate demand and aggregate supply curves. Hicks's IS-LM diagram is a better analogue of the Marshallian demand and supply diagram which generations of economists were familiar with than what Keynes had proposed (see Figure 3). He used this to show that there could be an equilibrium that could be short of full employment. He also showed how comparative static analysis could be carried out to show that policy would shift the equilibrium toward full employment.

Hicks's macroeconomic analogue of the Marshallian Cross had the rate of interest and the level of income on the two axes. The analogy with price (rate of interest) and quantity (income) is clear. The IS curve, like the demand curve, sloped downward from left to right, tracing the combinations of the rate of interest and income at which savings and investment would equal each other. The other curve LM traced an upward-rising relationship between rate of interest and income at which the demand and supply of money were in equilibrium. The intersection of the IS and LM curves determined the income level and the rate of interest. The income level was implicitly also able to convey the

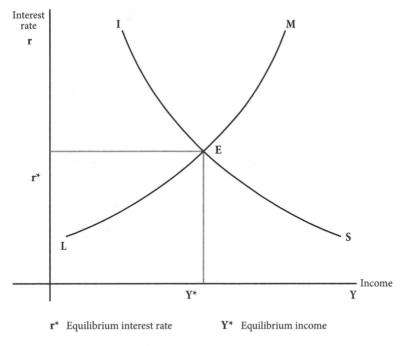

r* Equilibrium interest rate   Y* Equilibrium income

Figure 3 Hicks's version of Keynes: the IS-LM curves

level of employment. So one could have equilibrium at a level of income (employment) below the full potential income (full employment) level. If one could then manipulate the two policy variables implicit in the diagram – public spending to raise consumer spending to a higher level or money supply to lower interest rate and raise investment – you could illustrate how policy could be used to restore full employment. The only remaining task was for the econometricians to obtain the numbers to estimate the slopes of the IS and LM curves.

Hicks's triumph was complete. Economists no longer needed to wade through the *General Theory* and promptly stopped doing so. Keynes may have launched a revolution, but Hicks quickly domesticated his message and made it familiar to economists in terms they knew already. The emphasis was shifted from employment to income, from the labor market to the goods market. The entire problem of money wage rigidity was bypassed. Price level was taken as fixed. Later Franco Modigliani (Nobel Laureate 1985) added a labor market to the goods and money market, but that only elaborated on what was already a better summary.

It took the Keynesians some time before they began to feel uncomfortable in the Hicksian embrace. To begin with, everyone, including Keynes himself, welcomed Hicks's more palatable form. It enabled Keynes's message to be conveyed to many more economists. It was only later that some "fundamentalist" Keynesians began to protest that the original book had been ignored and the novelty of Keynes's argument obliterated in Hicks's version. Disagreements about Hicks's simplification of Keynes's model became rampant during the 1960s and 1970s, with large swathes of economists arguing that the IS-LM approach distorted the original message of Keynes's *General Theory*. Post-Keynesian economics was born in the 1960s, hoping to restore the true message of Keynes, but it remains a minority cult.

The Policy Legacy of Keynes

Yet, at the outset, there was much less disagreement about the effectiveness of Keynes's policy nostrums, or rather nostrums derived from his message by civil servants and Treasuries. This was more so in Anglo-Saxon economies than in continental European ones. In the UK especially, the Treasury, the bête noire of Keynes during much of his professional life, was won over completely. The notion of monetary policy being ineffective due to the liquidity trap became an accepted part of British policy. Fiscal policy – manipulation of public spending and budget deficits and surpluses – was taken to be central to all macro policy-making. Keynes's ideas led to legislation that set up "built-in stabilizers." Unemployment benefits, for example, ensured that even if unemployment rose the incomes of the unemployed did not fall precipitously, because benefits kicked in. Pensions were another stabilizer. It was the consumer who was the king. Investment was meant to follow passively. The priority for public policy was maintaining full employment.

Another idea that gained widespread appeal among policy-makers was that the level of public debt did not matter. Keynes held the view that the budget should be balanced over the cycle. Yet Keynes also thought that there was a longer run problem with capitalist societies. He was worried that depressions would recur because of excess savings in a rich society. Public debt was owned by the rentiers, who could hold society to ransom by refusing to let the rate of interest fall below a certain level. It was imperative to let the interest rate fall enough that there would be euthanasia of the rentier. During the immediate postwar period in the UK, as in the US, there was a drive to maintain very low interest rates. Tolerance of public debt was to be the hallmark of Keynesianism. When the first impulses to oppose Keynesian policies acquired political roots in the late 1950s and early 1960s, the focus was on the size of the public debt. In the US, extreme right-wing organizations such as the John Birch Society publicized the public debt as the cancer which was eating up American freedom. This idea has just got wider constituency in contemporary America.

Not every country took to Keynesian policies. In the arena of policy, the triumph of Keynesian economics was limited to the richer countries, and among them to Anglo-Saxon ones. Continental European economies – West Germany especially, recovering from war damage – pursued a much more orthodox monetary and fiscal policy, emphasizing savings and investment rather than consumption and public spending. Scandinavian economies had discovered Keynesian policies independently of Keynes, since the Stockholm School had pioneered many of the same ideas, which did not become better known until later. Keynes's message was declared to be unsuitable for poorer countries, some of which were just becoming independent. The Soviet bloc of countries never adopted Keynesian policies. Of course, economics textbooks everywhere used Keynesian ideas to teach macroeconomics.

In the US, initial enthusiasm for Keynesian policies lasted only until the end of the presidency of Harry Truman. In 1953, Eisenhower became the first Republican President since Herbert Hoover, in the 1930s, to be sworn into power. The two Democratic Presidents in between had pursued policies – the New Deal by Roosevelt especially – which, though not avowedly guided by Keynes's theories, aligned the Democratic Party with Keynesian policies. Under Eisenhower, fiscal policy became much more neutral. Although Eisenhower undertook the largest public investment program of any US President, either before him or since, neither he nor the chairman of his Council of Economic Advisers, Arthur F. Burns, believed that Keynesian activism was effective for short-run cyclical stabilization. The National Debt rose from $266 billion in 1953 to $286 billion in 1960, one of the lowest rates of increase in the postwar period and well below the rate of growth of GDP. The debt to GDP ratio did not rise during the Eisenhower years. The policy of a low interest rate was abandoned and fiscal prudence was prized. In the UK, a similar hardening of monetary policy took place when the Conservative Party displaced the Labour Party from power in 1951. The two major British political parties were not that far apart on this issue and a compromise emerged called Butskellism – a combination of the names of R. A. Butler, who was the Chancellor of the Exchequer for the governing Conservatives, and Hugh Gaitskell, who was the Shadow Chancellor and later Leader of the Labour Party. The US was to embrace Keynesian economics more fully when Kennedy became President in 1961 and implemented a tax cut in advance of a predicted recession. The recession was averted. It was after that significant piece of Keynesian policy that Richard Nixon, Kennedy's Republican rival in 1960 and President after 1969, uttered the now famous words: "I am now a Keynesian in economics." This made Keynesianism a bipartisan policy in the

US for the remainder of the 1970s. Fiscal policy remained the principal tool in the armory of policy-makers in Anglo-Saxon countries. But this was all to change in the 1980s.

The Highpoint of Keynesian Triumph

For 25 years after the end of World War II, the citizens of the developed countries enjoyed an unprecedented run of prosperity. There was full employment at a level that had not been seen since the 1920s. The unemployment rate in the UK was under 2 percent. The US, which calculates its unemployment rate differently, had it at 5 percent. Incomes grew year on year. A British worker employed in a factory aspired to work 48 weeks per year, 48 hours per week (including overtime) for 48 years of his working life. Sociologists were amazed to find that working-class people were renting homes subsidized from the public purse, and yet had cars parked outside which they owned. The Proletariat was being embourgeoisified!

Economic growth, which had previously been a theme of the classical economists, made a reappearance in economics. Roy Harrod, who was Keynes's first biographer, proposed in a series of lectures given at the LSE in 1948 that growth of income in an economy was a simple product of a savings ratio divided by a capital–output ratio.[6] Savings equaled investment and investment was an addition to the capital stock. The capital–output ratio provided a method for working out how much capital was required to produce an extra unit of income. Thus if investment was an addition to capital, dividing it by the capital–output ratio gave you the addition to income which resulted.

During the 1950s, economists began delving into historical statistics, including those of income, capital, and labor. This research led to discoveries of constants and regularities and as a result the capital–output ratio was found to be around 3. So if the economy saved and invested 15 percent of the national income, the resulting growth would be 5 percent (15 divided by 3). Growth, at least in the US economy, had been more or less continuous except for the years of the Depression. Robert Solow used the Cobb-Douglas production function to try and explain growth. To his astonishment, he found that if you valued the labor input at the real wage level and capital stock at its rental, the resulting income growth was only one-eighth of the total growth. Thus seven-eighths was unexplained – "residual." And so began the search to explain this residual, with economists eventually concluding that it was due to "technical progress." Workers were attaining higher levels of education and were healthier, and as a result more productive. Machines were getting smarter even while their prices were falling, thanks to research and development. It seemed that if only the economy could avoid unemployment, there would be continuous income growth. For many, Keynes had solved the problem of economic growth forever.

But, for others, Keynes had not fully explained the occurrence of business cycles. To be fair, he had, in chapter 22 of the *General Theory* "Notes on the Trade Cycle." But no one, however, had read that far and there has been no explicit recognition of his argument about the cycle. Keynes told the world that a capitalist economy could have two alternative states of equilibrium – one at full employment and the other at less than full employment. The economy might get stuck at the underemployment equilibrium for prolonged periods of time unless deliberately moved. The postwar data showed that the economy was cruising along at full employment. There were short lapses from full employment, but these were quickly corrected thanks to the "built-in" stabilizers – unemployment compensation, social security, old age pensions – which kept demand up even when unemployment was rising.

The result of the continuous full employment was that any interest in business cycles disappeared from academia just 20 years after Schumpeter had written his two-volume classic, *Business Cycles*. The view that business cycles of the prewar type were a thing of the past gained popularity. There would be small recessions which would be short-lived, but not cycles which the policy-makers could not control. In 1970, a collection of articles came out with the title *Is the Business Cycle Obsolete?*[7] It seemed prophetic, though it proved to be hasty.

During the 1950s and even into the 1960s, Keynesian economics informed the economic thinking of academics, especially of the generation born since 1920. It infected politicians as well. Anthony Crosland, a young British socialist, surmised in his book *The Future of Socialism* (1956) that with the scourge of unemployment eliminated and full employment and growth guaranteed, the idea of socialism could be made more attractive as one of sharing the fruits of growth more equitably and without the prospects of a grim class struggle as envisaged by the communists. Keynes's ideas on the threat posed by the "rich" through excessive savings and a resistance to low interest rates by the rentier class gave a boost to redistributive philosophy. Now redistribution was economically efficient as well as politically desirable for the left. John Kenneth Galbraith made his name with his bestseller *The Affluent Society* (1958), arguing that while private affluence was now a fact of life, public amenities needed a better allocation of resources.

The 1950s were the high point of Keynesian triumph. Cycles had been eliminated and economic growth seemed to be guaranteed. There was full employment and prosperity was more widely distributed than ever before. As Harold Macmillan, the British Prime Minister, told his electorate in 1957, "You never had it so good."[8]

But Was It Really All Due to Keynes?

A rough and ready history became popular in the 1950s. It went something like this. Before the Great Depression, Old Economics ruled the roost. It believed in the efficacy of free markets and the virtues of a balanced budget. Then came the Great Depression and Old Economics was at a loss to explain it. Indeed, it suggested more cuts in public spending and made the Depression worse. Then came Keynes, who had the solution and a New Economics.

Voila! the Depression was defeated and economists discarded the Old Economics and adopted the New. For many American economists of a certain age, the Roosevelt New Deal became identified with Keynesian economics.

However, in reality Keynes published the *General Theory* in 1936. By this time, incomes had begun to recover in both the US and UK. One of the main problems in economics is that numbers are forever getting revised. Thus it may be that the latest estimates of the income levels in the 1930s are rosier than the ones people felt they experienced then. Yet the evidence is impressive. The most recently available income data for the US show that GDP in the country rose year on year between 1918 and 1929 (except for 1921), and by 1929 income was 45 percent above its 1918 level. Then income fell from 1929 year on year till 1933, and by then it was 40 percent below the 1929 level, that is, just at the 1918 level. Then it began to rise. There was a slight fall of about 4 percent year on year in the year 1938 (later blamed by Keynesians on Roosevelt's desire to balance the budget), but income resumed its rise till 1941, the last prewar year. By 1941 the GDP had risen from its lowest level in 1931 by 80 percent. Over the years 1929–41 the increase was around 45 percent.

The British economy had a very different trajectory from the US economy. There was a very high rate of inflation in the immediate postwar years of 1919 and 1920. As we saw above the inflation rate was 20 percent. Incomes fell in three successive years, 1919, 1920 and 1921, and were 20 percent lower than their 1918 peak level. The next eight years saw a very weak recovery when incomes rose year on year (except for 1926) but had not reached their 1918 peak by 1929. But the Depression was short; just two years of fall in income –1930 and 1931 – and then growth resumed. By 1934, the 1918 level was exceeded. Thus the UK had a long period of a low or falling growth rate between 1918 and 1929, two years of severe depression, and then the 1918 level was regained by 1934. Thus if we date the Great Depression from 1929, by 1934 the UK economy was back at the 1918 level. From then on till 1939, the last prewar year (except for the last three months), income rose. Thus while there was a lot of social and political turmoil during the 1930s, the cold numbers of income (available long after the event, however) show a much brighter picture.

How do we explain the course of the economy during the 1930s? Was it the arrival of a new theory or just routine policy-making by governments who had to innovate? Governments did jettison old rules and adopt untried methods. Although Roosevelt fought his 1932 campaign on a balanced budget program, upon being elected he instigated legislative changes to create a vigorous set of programs aimed to provide public sector employment for the unemployed. In this, he anticipated the lesson of the *General Theory*. Keynes had also given lectures in the US, the most famous of which came out as a pamphlet under the title *The Means to Prosperity*. This contained his general message before he had fully worked out the academic infrastructure. But even so, the idea that in distressed times you launch public works to create jobs was hardly novel.

For a book written by an Englishman, the *General Theory* had ignored international trade and payments issues. The economy modeled in the *General Theory* is a closed economy. This was perhaps truer for America where trade – exports and imports – were a smaller proportion of GDP than for the UK. Even so, international developments had not been unimportant, either for Britain or the US. Here the changes in the Gold Standard became crucial. The British leadership of the Gold Standard had been ceded to the Americans when the British went into debt as a result of World War I. The US had the largest reserves of gold by 1918. Roosevelt had the power to change the price at which America would buy gold, and in 1933 he "devalued" the dollar by changing the gold price. Britain had already abandoned the Gold Standard in 1931 and devalued its currency. In Britain, the abandonment of the Gold Standard allowed the pursuit of a cheap money policy and short-term interest rates went below 2 percent, There was a building boom, which generated employment. Neville Chamberlain, who was Chancellor of the Exchequer at the time, kept the budget in balance. But he managed to convert Britain's high level of debt to a lower coupon (3.5 percent rather than 5 percent) by deft persuasion.[9] (The rentiers were reasonable after all.) Thus, while the debt to income ratio remained high (75 percent, mainly due to World War I), the servicing burden as a proportion of the budget fell by a half, thereby releasing money for spending. It was monetary policy which did much of the work, as well as devaluation of the pound sterling which boosted exports. Monetary and exchange rate policies, far from being ineffective, did the job for the UK. Britain also gained from a de facto protectionist policy by adopting Imperial Preference.

Thus, to give Keynes credit for the escape of the economy from depression would be to commit an anachronism, or at least an exaggeration. The cure for the Great Depression, much of which had ended before 1936, was perhaps more due to international exchange rate depreciation, and in Britain a loose monetary policy.

Renewal of Attack on Keynesian Economics

The postwar hegemony of Keynesian economics was complete in universities. At Harvard, Alvin Hansen became the proselytizer for Keynesian ideas. His students Paul Samuelson, James Tobin, James Duesenberry, and Lloyd Metzler went on to dominate postwar economics teaching in the US. Hansen stripped any subtlety from Keynes's theory even more than had Hicks. His famous Keynesian Cross diagram concentrated on the multiplier and tried to show how total expenditure – consumption determined by income and investment (taken to be given) – determined output. All you needed to know was a couple of straight lines. His students passed this on. Samuelson's textbook became a bestseller and through it most American economists were trained to be Keynesians in their macroeconomics. Samuelson's student Lawrence Klein, who had coined the term "the Keynesian Revolution," became known for translating

Keynesian ideas into econometric models, which could then be used for policy purposes.[10]

There was, however, a problem at the heart of economics. In microeconomics, the theory of single markets taken individually (partial equilibrium) or taken simultaneously (general equilibrium) was taught. Economists learnt that the market works, that is, that all markets clear and there is no excess supply left unsold or excess demand left unsatisfied at the end of the day. In macroeconomics, they learnt that the labor market often failed to clear and hence public policy was needed to correct that anomaly. The two strands seemed incompatible.

Walrasian or Marshallian economics did not face this problem. It had no need of a theory of aggregate output or employment. The total was the sum of the individual parts. At the economy-wide level, only the quantity theory was needed to fix the absolute level of prices. With Keynes came the problem of reconciling micro and macro. Keynes accepted, while laying out his case in chapter 2 of the *General Theory*, that parts of the neoclassical theory worked well. Thus, the employer demanding labor was quite correct to equate the marginal product to the real wage. The problem in his view was that the worker as a supplier of labor could not guarantee that the marginal disutility of work (as measured by the number of hours worked) would be equal similarly to the real wage. The worker had no way of forcing an equilibrium since the hours on offer might be fewer than those he wanted to work and he could not cut his real wage. This then was the principal, and indeed the only, chink in the neoclassical armor as Keynes tried to reason it. On this basis, and reckoning with the difficulty faced by the worker in cutting his real wage so as to equalize his marginal disutility to the wage, Keynes proposed an alternative – a more general theory of how employment was determined. Innovations such as the consumption function, while they spoke of individual behavior, were macroeconomic and were not related to microeconomic concepts such as demand curves or the utility functions of consumers. The marginal efficiency of capital was argued in terms of a single investor, but somehow aggregated for the economy as a whole.

Paul Samuelson (1915–2009), as the High Priest of economics (albeit at a very young age, being not yet 40 by 1950), cut through the Gordian knot and opined that Keynesian economics at a macro level gave us the tools to achieve full employment, which allowed micro economics come into its full play. This dichotomous, some would say schizophrenic, compromise was called the neoclassical-Keynesian synthesis.

The basic objections of the rejectionists were conceded. If you took microeconomics seriously, then Keynesian results would not hold unless there were wage rigidities. If Keynesian economics was to be valid, then different *microeconomic foundations* were required than were on offer in the *General Theory*. Post-Keynesians, who are fundamentalists and reject the Hicks formulation, rely on notions of imperfect competition to build micro foundations which are not strictly Walrasian and do not assume perfect competition. But they have not made much impact on the general debate. This may sound theological but there were real political undercurrents at play. A Keynesian would allot an active role to the state to regulate the market. The rejectionist was wedded to the classical notion of laissez-faire.

Keynesian Economics in Action

Keynes's theory lent itself easily to a mathematical formulation. During World War II, scientific research had been harnessed to the war effort. The idea that government policy could be improved by using modern tools of mathematics and statistics was central to both the war effort and postwar policy-making. If so, the parameters of the relationships derived in Keynes's theory, such as the marginal propensity to consume or the accelerator, could be estimated from historical data and used to guide future policy. Econometrics itself was a developing subject in those days and computing power was slowly increasing. Keynesian economists could promise statistical sophistication to policy-makers. (Keynes himself was skeptical about the use of these statistical tools, but his objections were ignored.)

The American Keynesians faced an immediate setback. As World War II drew to a close, they made dire predictions on the state of the economy. Based on the intuitive assumptions that government spending would be drastically reduced and that swathes of soldiers returning from the war would face unemployment, they forecast that a negative multiplier would come into play, which would result in a sizable reduction in output. But, as it turned out, there was a boom. People had been exhorted to save during the war, and indeed there had been very little to spend money on. Once the war ended, men and women got married and formed households. They had money to buy houses and refrigerators and radios and cars. The money balances available to spend lifted the economy and this continued until 1949. In a sense, this vindicated Pigou's insight about money balances playing a crucial role in moving the economy up. Keynesians had to do better in predicting the workings of the economy.

But the econometricians were not dejected by this initial setback. The Cowles Foundation was the incubator for new developments in econometrics and there the first models of the US economy were estimated by Lawrence Klein (who won the Nobel Prize in 1980). They were based on annual data for income, consumption, investment, and employment. From small beginnings – the first model had only six equations – econometric models grew in size. By 1955, Klein, along with his associate Arthur Goldberger, had built a 20-equation model. These models were dominated by quantitative relationships among income and expenditure. Prices and interest rates played a minor part or no part at all in explaining the workings of the economy. The Keynesian orthodoxy about the irrelevance of money was maintained by these models. Their use for informing policy debates continued and by the early 1960s the American Social Science Research Council had invested financial and personnel resources to enable a larger model to be devised in which many US universities cooperated. The Brookings-SSRC Econometric Model of the US Economy had scores of equations.

One issue was to ask whether Keynesian models could mimic the cyclical behavior of the US economy. The data underlying the models spanned much of the early twentieth century and so it was reasonable to ask whether the models could reproduce the cycles. In 1959 Frank Adelman, a physicist, and his wife, Irma Adelman, an economist, carried out the first computer simulation of the Klein-Goldberger model to see whether the models reproduced the cycles.[11] It turned out not to be the case. The model, when subjected to random shocks, showed that mild cycles could be generated in the model but the cycles soon died down. The Adelmans' innovative method for generating random shocks within a computerized model became the template for subsequent simulations.

The Adelmans had shown that the economy when depicted by a Keynesian model was not structured like a bouncy rocking horse as demonstrated by Ragnar Frisch's analogy. It had to be jolted again and again to generate up and down movements. This might be a consequence of Keynes's theory being faulty, or perhaps the way it had been translated into algebra and later into a model. That would require a fundamental rethinking of the whole project. Alternatively, it could be that better models were required. This was the line taken by economists involved in modeling. They saw this as an additional challenge. Models went on being built on a larger and larger scale to capture the minutiae of the economy. Of course, there was also the fact that the postwar period had hardly recorded any deep cycles. Recessions were infrequent and short-lived thanks to

Keynesian policies, or so at least the mainstream economists thought.

The Specter of Inflation

The Achilles heel of Keynesian policy was inflation. This became a problem increasingly in the 1950s and 1960s. Keynesian models neglected prices as they also downplayed the role of money. Unemployment was the real and persistent danger in the world of Keynesian economics. The manner in which Hicks and Hansen had expounded Keynes's theory meant that prices were taken as fixed. In the *General Theory* itself, Keynes had taken the money wage as given for the first 18 chapters while he laid out his new theory. In chapters 19 to 21 he had proceeded to work out the effects of changes in money wages and prices on his argument. But no one read the whole book anymore. The summaries of Hicks and Hansen were the gospel truth. Thus the entire subject of inflation, which became a growing reality from the late 1950s onward, surprised the Keynesians.

The rejectionists had been waiting for such an event and pounced. As orthodox economists, they championed not only laissez-faire but also the quantity theory of money, which could explain inflation. Keynes had rejected the quantity theory as irrelevant for economies with mass unemployment. At full employment, he did acknowledge that the quantity theory would come into its own. Describing how the economy would behave if it got close to full employment, he wrote "We have reached ... a situation (i.e. full employment) in which the crude quantity theory of money (interpreting 'velocity' to mean 'income-velocity') is fully satisfied; for output does not alter and prices rise in exact proportion to MV."[12]

But his followers would have none of it. Money for them was a passive variable in driving the economy, and prices were determined not by money but by production costs. The 1960s witnessed a classic confrontation between the Keynesians and the rejectionists. Orthodox economics had been reinvigorated as a result of the efforts of Milton Friedman (1912–2006), who had established a formidable research base at the University of Chicago to rebut Keynesian orthodoxies. The counterattack was systematic and nuanced, using the best techniques familiar to the Keynesians and demolishing the pillars of Keynesian economics one by one, starting with the consumption function. Much of this counterattack occurred while I was a graduate student in the early 1960s and during my early years as a professional economist. The debates generated around Friedman's work were intense, almost passionate, because every one taking part in them knew that they were not debating just technical issues but questions of the kind of politics needed to guide economic policy.

Friedman subjected Keynes's basic idea of the consumption function to a rigorous statistical test in his book *A Theory of the Consumption Function* (1957). He examined the annual time series of consumption and income, but also family budget data for several separate years. He concluded that Keynes's basic proposition – that the marginal propensity to consume (MPC) was less than one and declined as income rose – was flawed. Families spent a constant proportion of their permanent income rather than their actual income. They gauged their permanent income by taking into account their savings and wealth positions as well as their current income. The policy implication was that the multiplier would be much smaller than the Keynesians had assumed if, given a sudden dollop of income, households would treat it like a windfall and save it rather than consume it. Thus, having undermined one pillar of Keynesian economics, Friedman's next coup was to challenge the primacy of the multiplier as a determinant of income movements and argue for the importance of money supply.

Friedman argued that the movements of national income in nominal terms – without correcting for inflation – were better explained by movements in money supply than by autonomous investment, that is, the multiplier process. Keynesians had argued that money did not matter and could not be relied upon as a policy tool. It was autonomous investment mainly derived from the public budget which, via the multiplier, determined where the economy would be in terms of high or low income. Friedman, with his co-author David Meiselman, wrote a paper that was based on employing econometric analysis on twentieth-century data on the American economy.[13] It showed that equations using money supply as an explanatory variable had more statistical power than equations using autonomous investment. There was also a difference in the methodology used. While Keynesians were building larger models, Friedman and

Meiselman used a single equation for each of the two hypothesis – investment or money supply. They then compared the performance of the two equations in terms of explanatory power over the same sample. By this method, they demonstrated that the equation using money supply as an explanatory variable performed better than the one using autonomous investment.

Friedman's triumph caused a fierce debate among American economists on the usefulness of rival equations and models. As a young graduate student, I witnessed the fury of my Keynesian teachers and their friends about the result they were confronted with. The Keynesians questioned the statistical details and also the lack of complexity in Friedman's model. Eventually, they conceded the statistical point.[14] Yet the question remained of explaining the reasons for the better performance. The ways in which money supply influenced income – the transmission mechanism – had yet to be elaborated, according to the Keynesians. Once again Friedman had dented, if not shaken, a pillar of the Keynesian edifice. Henceforth Keynesians had to include the influence of money in their models. A new effort was initiated by the Federal Reserve Board along with the Massachusetts Institute of Technology and the University of Pennsylvania (FRB-MIT-PENN model) to build a larger model to investigate the transmission mechanism. Yet even then Friedman was not done with the Keynesians. His next attack was on the issue of what caused inflation.

Here, paradoxically, the Keynesians took the microeconomic route and argued that unit labor costs (wages divided by labor productivity) determined prices of individual products. Producers added a profit markup to unit costs and determined prices. Milton Friedman and his associates argued that it was the total money supply in the economy which determined the general price level. If money supply did not accommodate the higher costs and prices, some businesses would close. Only those firms which had competitive unit labor costs would survive. In the absence of an accommodative money supply, there would then be no inflation.

The inflation gap in the Keynesian theory was filled by Phillips's work on wage inflation and unemployment. A. W. H. Phillips (1914–75) was brought up on a dairy farm in New Zealand. In 1937 he went to China and escaped just ahead of the Japanese invasion. Reaching Britain, he studied electrical engineering, and then, at the outbreak of World War II, signed up for the Royal Air Force. Within days of Japan declaring hostilities, he was flown to Singapore, which fell almost as soon as Phillips arrived. He managed to escape to Java, but when that too was overrun, he was captured and spent the rest of the war in a Japanese prison camp. Being a man of ingenuity, he was able to construct a radio to receive BBC broadcasts. He also taught himself Chinese with the help of a fellow prisoner and could read up to two hundred Chinese characters.

When the war was over, Phillips joined the LSE, where he followed a non-specialist degree in the social sciences. To understand Keynesian theory better, he put his engineering skills to good use and built a hydraulic analogue model of the economy, the first such model to be constructed. One of the professors at the LSE, James Meade (a Nobel Prize winner in 1977 for his contribution to international trade), saw the model, which was in Phillips's garage. Impressed by this innovation, he offered Phillips a fellowship to research ways in which to regulate the working of an economy on the principles of a servomechanism, which uses error-sensing feedback to improve performance. Phillips did some pioneering work in devising policy rules using control theory.

He made his name, however, by studying the historical record of unemployment and the course of money wage rates for the period 1861–1913. His results were published as an article in 1958.[15] In these 52 years he found that across the six and a half cycles lasting eight years on average, as unemployment fell wage rates rose faster, and vice versa. There was a bottom below which money wage rates would not fall no matter how high unemployment went. This provided weak support for the idea of money wage rigidity. But there was a clear relationship between money wage rate rises and unemployment, which sloped downward like a demand curve but formed more of an L shape (see Figure 4). For later periods the association was not as strong. The interwar period had witnessed levels of unemployment that were unprecedented by pre–1914 standards, and post–1945 there was little variation in the level of unemployment as governments were wedded to a Keynesian policy. Researchers in the UK and US took up the task of estimating the "Phillips curve" using contemporary data. Paul Samuelson and his MIT colleague

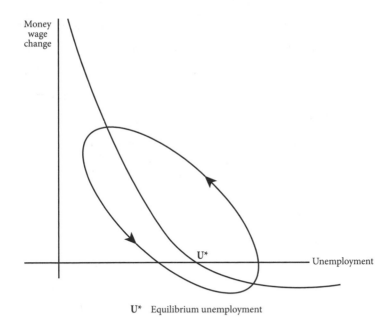

U*   Equilibrium unemployment

Figure 4 The Phillips curve

Robert Solow, two of the foremost US economists, presented a paper entitled "Analytical Aspects of an Anti-Inflation Policy" before the American Economic Association Conference in 1959.[16] This was perceived as an official seal of approval to the Phillips curve as a policy tool.

Phillips had provided Keynesians with the answer to what caused prices to rise: inflation. Persistently high levels of employment led to sustained money wage rises, and hence, by implication, via unit labor costs, price rises. Inflation was a labor market phenomenon, not a monetary one. The Phillips curve gave policy-makers a new tool but it involved making an uncomfortable choice. If the curve showed that at 3 percent unemployment, wage inflation was 10 percent, but at 5 percent unemployment, it was only 6 percent, the policy choice was clear: increase unemployment to 5 percent. Depending on the nature of the economy, the answer was to keep the economy at that level of unemployment which would slow down the rise in wages and hence the rise in prices. This level of unemployment was labeled by Phillips's LSE colleague Frank Paish as "slack" in the economy. There seemed to be a "trade-off" between the level of unemployment and the rate of inflation. For those who did not like the policy of raising the unemployment level, the solution was to secure the cooperation of trade unions and employers in restraining wage rises. Thus were born the "incomes policies" which were tried as anti-inflation tools during the 1970s. Inflation, though, continued to pose a major challenge to the Keynesians.

The battle was now on between the Keynesians and the rejectionists, who were now labeled monetarists. It was fought as much through equations and econometrics as through prose. Milton Friedman took up the cudgel on behalf of monetarism. He challenged the claim that the Phillips curve was, either analytically or as a policy tool, a good idea. This counterattack from Friedman and Chicago concentrated on the fragility of the Phillips curve. It honed in on the inconsistency with neoclassical theory, which held that demand and supply depended on relative and not absolute prices, that is, real wages and not money wages in the labor market. He offered instead a superior explanation based on the movements in money stock.[17]

Friedman began with a deconstruction of the Phillips curve, which had been made the principal weapon in the official Keynesian policy armory. He argued that if the curve reflected the wage bargaining process, then it was incomplete. Workers would be interested in their real wage not their money wage. Their demand for a money wage increase would be influenced by their expectations of inflation. The Phillips curve would shift rightward and upward as inflation persisted (see Figure 5). If the rate of inflation was 3 percent, workers might be happy with a 6 percent increase in money wages. But, if it were 5 percent they would

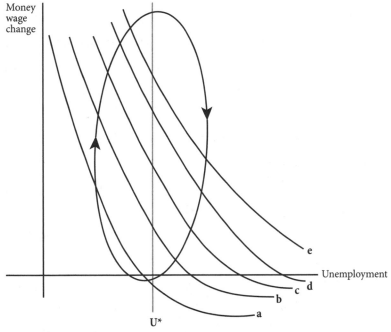

U* Natural rate of unemployment

Figure 5 Friedman's version of the Phillips curve: as expected inflation rises, the curve shifts upward from a to e

demand 8 percent at a given level of unemployment. To control inflation, one could not use the Phillips curve as a device since the curve itself shifted because of the level of inflation. There was also the question of whether the aggregate level of unemployment could be determined by the government. Friedman argued on the basis of neoclassical theory that the aggregate level of unemployment would be the result of many separate labor markets in different sectors. Following Wicksell's term, natural rate of interest, Friedman called this market-determined level of unemployment the natural rate of unemployment. Governments trying to aim for a lower level than the natural one would cause inflation, and a higher one would depress the economy.

Friedman challenged the Phillips curve in his presidential address to the American Economic Association in December 1967. It was published in March 1968 and sounded the death knell of policy prescriptions based on the Phillips curve.[18] By the end of the 1960s, the Keynesians had accepted that the consumption function should include the influence of "permanent income" rather than just current income, the investment function had been adapted to show the impact of interest rates, and money supply had to be included as an important variable in determining the course of the economy. But there was much worse to come for the Keynesians. Over the course of the next decade and a half, the reception given to Friedman's ideas changed. By the end of the 1960s, his ideas were taken as a serious challenge to be met. By the mid-1970s, Friedman had become the most influential economist.

Having dealt with the consumption function, the multiplier and the Phillips curve, Friedman moved on to provide an alternative paradigm for macroeconomics. This was monetarism. Monetarism derived much of its argument from the Cambridge equation of money demand on which Keynes had done much work before he wrote the *General Theory*. It shifted the policy focus away from fiscal policy and toward money supply, and linked the budget deficits with loss of control over money supply.

At Chicago, Friedman had inaugurated a research program in the demand for money and the study of hyperinflations through history. This was to undermine the weakness in the received Keynesian theory. The Chicago School argued that the quantity theory was a theory of the demand for money based on the use of money for transactions and precautionary purposes. This linked the Chicago tradition to the pre-*General Theory* Cambridge tradition of Marshall and Pigou and their work on the holding of money balances. Using this tradition, the demand for money was substantially linked to nominal income. This contrasted with Keynes's theory of the demand for money, which focused largely on the speculative motive and the role of interest rates. Keynes had himself abandoned the Cambridge tradition in which he was such a major player.

The other strand of Chicago was to emphasize the role of expectations. Keynes had also emphasized the role of expectations in his theory. Short-term expectations determined the output decisions of the producer, and long-term expectations influenced by "animal spirits" determined investment. Keynes had not translated these ideas into algebra; indeed he believed long-term expectations could not be determined by rational procedures. The Chicago School used the idea of "adaptive expectations" to study people's reaction to inflation. Adaptive expectations are predicated on the idea that our expectations of what will happen tomorrow are based on an average of today's events and those of the recent past. If inflation has been creeping up, we would expect it to go on rising further. We would then bring our purchases forward to avert the higher prices; but that would make prices more likely to rise further. During the German hyperinflation, this adaptive behavior occurred during the course of the day so that by the afternoon prices were higher than they had been in the morning.

Monetarism undermined the twin pillars of Official Keynesianism. Budget deficits were no longer benign and inflation rather than underemployment was the principal problem market economies had to tackle.

Chapter Five

DECLINING FORTUNES

When World War II was coming to an end and the outcome was certain, attention turned to postwar economic issues. Continental Europe had been subjected to large-scale destruction during the war. Britain had emerged as a joint victor with the US, but even so its economy was hard-pressed to provide prosperity. The US alone had fought and won the war without too much privation to its citizens. Even so, everyone dreaded a return to depression. In this context Keynesian policies delivered 25 years of full employment between 1945 and 1970 for the American economy. Western Europe was to receive Marshall Aid, which was also a Keynesian idea since donating the money to war-torn Europe was helpful for American exports. This enabled Western Europe to reconstruct without too much unemployment and return to prosperity by the late 1950s.

America had the largest reserve of gold and was the most powerful economy. While World War II was still raging, preparations were made for the postwar economic order. The outbreak of protectionism during the Depression had been bad for the world and the new order would push as much as possible for free trade. It would form one of the three pillars of the postwar economic order. But there was also a desire to avoid the anarchy that had followed the abandonment of the Gold Standard, with countries devaluing their currencies to the detriment of other nations. Add to this the overwhelming determination to avoid the mass unemployment and misery of the Great Depression from ever repeating itself and you had a pretty heavy agenda.

Negotiations for postwar currency arrangements were carried out at Bretton Woods. The Allied delegations met to discuss proposals by Keynes, representing the UK, and Harry White, representing the US. Other Allied countries played a minor walk-on part. Keynes had the ambitious plan of creating a common currency for the world. He wanted to establish a banking facility where the trade surpluses of all trading countries would be deposited. The surpluses would then be loaned out to countries with trade deficits. Keynes dreaded the repetition of the experience where deficit countries had to reduce domestic demand in order to reduce imports and had to lower their prices to export more in order to correct their trade imbalance. He believed that countries running surplus should make an equal effort at importing more, whereby their surpluses would go down and help the deficit countries to export more.

The Americans, who were going to be the sole surplus country in the immediate postwar period, did not fancy being compelled to adapt their policy to outside diktats. Keynes's version of the Bretton Woods system was not accepted in its entirety. Keynes's plan of creating a common currency for the world was also not acceptable in the circumstances. At Bretton Woods, instead of the Gold Standard, the outcome was the dollar exchange standard, with the dollar's value fixed in terms of gold. The US agreed to buy and sell gold at $35 an ounce, as the Bank of England had done before World War I (at £3 17s 10½d). But gold was not to circulate domestically, nor would citizens be allowed to present gold bullion for coinage.

It was decided to have a system of fixed exchange rates, with the dollar as the reserve currency. All currencies had to declare and defend a fixed parity with the dollar. The International Monetary Fund was established to police the working of the fixed exchange rate standard. The IMF was allowed to give loans to countries in temporary balance-of-payments difficulty, but only if they promised to correct the imbalance by suitable deflation, or, in extreme cases, devaluation.

The structure of fixed exchange rates in a dollar exchange standard entailed restricted capital movements. Keynes saw this as crucial, not only in general terms as a way of preserving a full employment policy, but also as a protective wall for the UK, which was to emerge quite impoverished in capital asset terms after the war. These restrictions meant that a government had more control over its international payments than was the case with the Gold Standard. Governments also had control over their own money supply as long as their trade deficits were not so large as to cause a run on their currency and a likely devaluation. Britain tried to maintain its status as a victorious Allied power and retained sterling as a reserve currency, but within 25 years of 1945 sterling had to be devalued twice. Only the dollar was the true reserve currency. The shelter of a fixed exchange rate, control over their own money supply, and the relaxed attitude about budget deficits and public debt allowed Western economies to have 25 years of steady growth with only a few shallow recessions.

Inflation was a problem but until the end of the 1960s it was mainly a domestic problem which different countries dealt with in their own way. The Bretton Woods system had laid down certain constraints within which macroeconomic policy had to operate. For the UK, the narrow limits between preserving the convertibility of sterling at par and fear of unemployment becoming unpopularly large meant that the policy was one of Stop-Go. The economy operated at full employment as far as possible, but if it overheated and the balance of trade showed a deficit that brought forth an attack on sterling by foreign investors, the government then slammed on the breaks. Unemployment would rise from, say, 1.5 percent to 2.5 percent and soon there would be cries for reflation and the economy was on the Go track again.

The US had a pretty robust growth period with full employment after the war. Except for the two mild recessions in 1949 and 1957, the economy boomed. In the early years of John F. Kennedy's presidency, econometric models predicted that a third recession might be coming, and a tax cut was proposed. It was enacted soon after Kennedy's death by Lyndon B. Johnson. This was the first example of a preemptive tax cut to avert a predicted recession. It succeeded.

But the economy went into overdrive. President Johnson had expanded the welfare state as part of his Great Society crusade. On the international front, the US was fighting a war in Vietnam and maintaining a large defense budget due to the Cold War. Soon its trade deficit became very large. Creditor countries that had previously been happy to hold dollars in their reserves were no longer pliant. France became the first country to exercise the option that the US sell gold in return for dollars. Once this happened, the stability of the dollar's value was called into question.

The outflow of gold could not be sustained but nor could US stop spending on the Vietnam War. Therefore, on August 15, 1971, President Nixon announced that the US was reneging on its promise to exchange dollars for gold at $35 an ounce. (This was a similar approach to the abandonment of gold in 1799 by the Bank of England and the issuance of paper currency.)

For the first time in nearly 300 years, there was neither gold nor a gold-based anchor to guide nations as to how much money to issue. Each country was free to print as much of its currency as its policy would permit. Once the constraints were relaxed, there came the problem of finding domestic anchors for an anti-inflation policy. This meant that the money of a country, while being a unit of account and a means of payment, became a risky store of value. Foreign exchange dealers were a small, specialized community in the days of Bretton Woods. They now became a much bigger presence in financial markets. Currencies had to be exchanged for trade purposes, of course, but also wealth needed to be guarded against erosion due to loss of value because of inflation and depreciation. Investors wanted to be able to move their assets from one currency to another quickly and cheaply. There were rich pickings here for the financial markets.

Once fixed exchange rates were replaced by flexible exchange rates, the dollar became the sole anchor for the international monetary system. This gave enormous seigniorage privilege to the US. Every country wanted to hold dollars as reserves since dollars were universally acceptable in trade, and indeed all prices were quoted in dollar terms. This allowed the US to issue more dollars relative to its income than would be the case for other economies. This was the privilege that European nations could not enjoy and complained about. But John Connally, the US Treasury Secretary under Nixon, famously summed up the US's response: "The dollar is our currency and your problem."

Around that time, telephones became much cheaper and much faster. The first commercial communications satellite had been launched and that made phone calls cheap and fast. The main beneficiaries of this development were foreign exchange (forex) dealers and stockbrokers. The multiplication of forex transactions took people by surprise. Early on during these developments, James Tobin (1918–2002), a distinguished economist at Yale and a Nobel Prize winner in 1981, proposed a tax on each forex transaction to slow down the hectic pace of the dealings. The world had never before seen so many currencies being required to carry on trade, and in which bonds and equities and other financial assets could be bought and sold. Tobin's proposal is still being debated after 40-plus years.

The Oil Shock

Just at this juncture, inflation became a global problem. Decades of persistent full employment had strengthened the trade unions and made the wage demands of workers irresistible. There had been a notion for many years before World War II that the share of wages in total national income was constant. The work of Paul Douglas had given support to this idea. Now the wage share began to drift up and the share of profit declined. Inflation was in one way a tranquilizer to ease the problem of the struggle between labor and capital for share in final income. Indeed the debate about the Phillips curve can be understood in this way. Could the workers be fobbed off with just nominal wage rises which could then be clawed back by inflation?

The price of oil had not risen for nearly 50 years up until 1973. The Arab-Israeli War was one proximate reason for the oil shock. But the persistence of inflation meant that the purchasing power of the dollar, in which oil was priced, was eroding as far as oil exporters were concerned. The quadrupling of the price of oil in October 1973 was partly a political gesture, but it had a profound economic impact in terms of both theory and practice.

Cheap oil, which had been available for nearly 50 years, had encouraged an energy-intensive technology to be built up for production as well as consumption (cars, refrigerators, air conditioners, washing machines). The rise in the price of oil increased costs of manufacturing, which were passed on to consumers in the form of higher prices. Dependence on imports for oil supplies meant that the developed economies had to transfer as much as 5 percent of their GDP to oil-exporting countries. Even as their imports became expensive, the rich countries' exports were being priced out of the market.

A side effect of the "oil shock" was felt by the financial system. The oil-exporting economies had limited scope for spending their newfound wealth. To begin with they chose to leave their wealth as bank deposits. Western banks found themselves flush with deposits. But to service them, they needed to loan them out and earn some interest. Much of this money went to developing countries that had up until then relied on intergovernmental loans: foreign aid. Now they could access bank loans. Banks believed that since these borrowers were sovereign states, there was no risk in lending to them. They were to learn their lesson later.

In theory, economists understand the interconnections between trade and finance and banking and credit creation. But as a subject, macroeconomics was taught and debated in terms of a closed economy, with only a small walk-on part for trade. Finance was discussed only in relation to public finance and government bonds. The private equity and bond markets and the commercial credit created by banks were ignored. Walrasian economics visualized barter as the principal way of allocation, and money played just an epiphenomenal part in general equilibrium. The reality, however, was one of open economies, multiple currencies, international trade and finance, and forex markets. There was no theory to cope with these new facts. Neither Keynesian theory nor monetarism looked beyond the closed economy.

Stagflation and the Return of Unorthodox Economics

Economics aims to be a science. Yet political events constantly change its agenda. The collapse of the Bretton Woods settlement as a consequence of American overspending and inflation exposed all the economies to the risks of inflation, which they struggled to control. The 1970s introduced the world to the concept of *stagflation*, an idea that the Phillips curve version of Keynesianism could not accommodate. There was simultaneously inflation and unemployment.

Keynesian economics had no theory or cure for inflation. The Phillips curve had been shown to be inconsistent with micro theory. In any case, the rate of inflation was too high for governments to use high unemployment as a weapon to bring it down. Governments tried to orchestrate voluntary agreements between trade unions and employers to moderate wage demands and slow price rises down. When voluntary agreements failed, they tried legislative means. Neither way worked. Governments also did not collect enough tax revenue to spend in a Keynesian fashion. Deficits, rare during the boom period of 1945–65, became endemic. Western countries were in fiscal crisis.

Monetarists were clamoring for a reduction in the deficit as a means of controlling the money supply. This meant controlling government spending rather than expanding it to bring unemployment down. It was at this juncture that Keynesian theories lost ground not only in academia but also in politics. The 1970s saw the rise of politicians of the right who were dedicated to cutting the money supply and restraining state spending as a way of curing the problems of stagflation. Margaret Thatcher, Ronald Reagan and Helmut Kohl sounded the death knell of the Keynesian consensus.

It was in this decade that the ideas of Hayek came back into fashion. There was also a revival of Marxian notions. Not so much in academia as in popular debate. Marxists had been marginalized because Keynes was reputed to have cured capitalism of its recurring crises. Instead of the workers being impoverished, they were prospering with full employment and high wages. Now with a crisis of high inflation and rising unemployment – stagflation – Marxists critiques became more widely read.

The Marxists were faced with the challenge of explaining the Keynesian era of capitalist prosperity without cycles or crises. Ernest Mandel, a Belgian Marxist, was the most articulate writer on the subject in the 1960s and 1970s. In an essay published in 1964, he argued that the world was going through the upward phase of a long Kondratieff cycle, which had an average duration of around 50 years.[1] The years between 1913 and 1939 had been the downward phase and the years from 1940s onward were the upward phase. The causes of the upward phase were the leaps made in technological innovation as a result of World War II and the Cold War, which made a whole new set of consumer durables affordable for middle-class consumers; a demographic bulge thanks to the Baby Boom which had generated the demand for the consumer durables; and the influx of labor from agriculture to industry which had been inaugurated by the Great Depression, leading to sustained high wage incomes as productivity rose thanks to technological innovations. These separate factors thus interacted with each other to guarantee that in the immediate postwar period, booms were long and recessions short.

In any event, Keynesians believed they had abolished the business cycle and not much credence was given to Mandel's analysis. Long cycles of the Kondratieff variety were a popular idea on the left but derided in academic economics. However, Mandel's predictions of the phases of the cycles bear an uncanny resemblance to reality. Written at the height of the years of Keynesian prosperity, Mandel's analysis of cycles predicted that the upward phase would end sometime in the early 1970s, as it did. As we saw in Chapter 2 above, Kondratieff had timed the Long Depression of the nineteenth century as starting in

1870/1875, ending the boom which had begun in 1844/51. The parallel to the dates in the twentieth century is uncanny.

While Kondratieff's long cycles were explained by a host of factors, the crucial problem was of the turning point from boom into bust. Marx, as we saw in Chapter 2, had a theory of why capitalism has crises and cycles. Indeed, his theory said that capitalism develops through cycles and crises. The source of the problem was the struggle between labor and capital over shares in income. Marx envisaged a cycle whereby, as the boom proceeded, labor markets got tighter and wages rose faster than productivity. The rate and share of profit then declined. This meant some businesses losing out, which is typical in a recession, with others adopting labor-replacing machinery. This slowed down wage rises and profits rose again. Once again, boom was restored to resume the next cycle. But Marx's works were not being much studied in academia.

Profitability had been eliminated from economic theory as a subject of interest. Profits were zero in equilibrium and neither the neoclassical nor the Keynesian economists worried much about profits or the profit rate. Andrew Glyn and Robert Sutcliffe in 1971 were the first to spot that the share of profit in the UK was falling, as was the rate of profit by the early 1970s, as a result of persistent full employment and powerful trade unions.[2] Inflation was just a symptom of this crisis of profitability. Workers were winning high rates of increase in money wages. The capitalists could claw back some of this rise by inflation of the product price. But that did not fool the workers when inflation became seriously high and persistent. They in return asked for higher wage rises. That process raised the share of wages and lowered the share and the rate of profits. Eventually, it was the fall in the rate of profit that had turned the upward phase of the Kondratieff cycle into its downward phase.

Glyn and Sutcliffe had caught the trend in wage share perfectly. It had risen in the UK from the mid-1950s to the early 1970s and reached a peak in 1975. This was also the year in which the UK experienced its highest ever rate of inflation – 25 percent. Academic economists did not take much notice, though Glyn was a Fellow at Oxford and Sutcliffe was teaching at Kingston Polytechnic then. They also predicted the consequences of the profit squeeze. Capital began migrating out to Asia during the 1970s and the UK began deindustrializing. This was to have a long-lasting effect on the structure of the UK economy. Similar trends were noticed in the US in the Northeast region at the same time. These economies began to become more service based and the income distribution became more unequal as the previously employed manual workers in manufacturing now became unemployed and unemployable, or had to take lower paid service jobs. The US economy went through the same cycle, with the wage share rising during the 1960s, peaking and then declining after 1975.

Academic macroeconomists did not see the significance of the declining wage share. There had been an attempt at the beginning of the Keynesian macro-modeling saga by Lawrence Klein to see whether the marginal propensity to consume out of wage income was larger than that out of non-wage income. It was, but once income got aggregated into a single number, the wage/profit distinction was abandoned. Of course, the political climate discouraged such class-based distinctions of income among the Americans. The witch hunt against communists started by Senator Joseph McCarthy affected academia and the arts more than many other sectors. While he was at teaching at the University of Michigan in the early 1950s, Lawrence Klein had come under suspicion of being a communist and had to exile himself to Oxford in the mid-1950s. He came back to the US in the late 1950s. By then the wage/profit distinction had been forgotten in macroeconomics.

A century after Marx wrote his opus *Capital*, in which he put forward his theory of the struggle for shares between capital and labor, Richard Goodwin (1913–96), an American-born Cambridge economist, encapsulated this theory into a game of rabbits and foxes. If there are too many rabbits, then foxes find their food easily and multiply. But then they exhaust the stock of rabbits and starve. As the numbers of foxes diminish, the rabbits have a time to grow again. But then life gets easier for foxes, and so on. (He adapted a mathematical model proposed by Vito Volterra and Alfred Lotka, who were studying the biology of fish populations which prey on other fish.) An "equilibrium" can be found by mathematical argument which would tell you the right proportion for the populations of rabbits and foxes. By analogy, the economy may have just the right distribution of the shares of labor and of capital. But unless by some accident the economy starts with those proportions, it will never get there from any other combination.[3] The essence of the model is that there is a long-run equilibrium with stable profit share and profit rate and constant shares of labor and capital. At the equilibrium we have the natural rate of employment (see Figure 6) and the equilibrium share (and by implication rate) of profit. Yet while there is an equilibrium "in theory," it is never reached if the economy starts at any point away from equilibrium. The economy goes around in a cycle perpetually without ever reaching an equilibrium. These

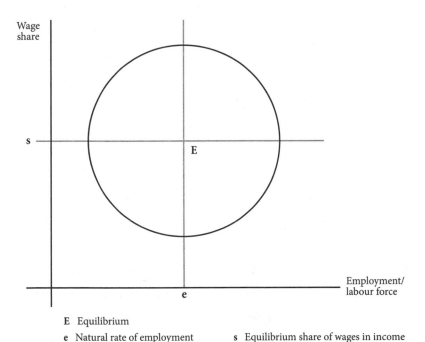

E Equilibrium
e Natural rate of employment   s Equilibrium share of wages in income

Figure 6 The Goodwin cycle

cycles can in principle be as long as 20 or 30 years depending on the parameters of the equations.

This insight is profoundly un-Keynesian as well as un-neoclassical. But it is informative. However, even this way of looking at the world was not fully global, as Marx would have wished. Stagflation resulted in the deindustrialization of the developed economies and the industrialization of what were hitherto developing economies. They were soon to be called the newly industrialized economies. Taiwan, South Korea, Hong Kong, and Singapore were called the Asian Tigers. They were followed by Malaysia, Indonesia, Thailand, and finally in the 1980s, China. Capital migrated from the West, where labor had become expensive, to Asia, the land of cheap labor, in search of higher profits. Many of the industrial products with standard technology were relocated abroad. The share of manufacturing in GDP and wage share declined in most major Western economies.

The stagflation at home was, however, still viewed in closed economy terms. It was here that the ideas of Hayek became popular again. Hayek had been Keynes's rival in the 1930s but it was believed that he had been proved to be wrong and Keynes right. His ideas survived in intense intellectual ghettoes. Hayek had, however, warned about the inflationary consequences of adopting Keynesian policies of perpetual reflation. Now, with stagflation as a phenomenon that was defeating the Keynesians, his ideas were taken seriously. Hayek had based his theory of the cycle on Wicksell's ideas. Booms were caused by cheap credit and later turned into slumps when banks panicked and raised interest rates. Reflation was the wrong policy to adopt in a slump because it was excess credit that had caused the crisis in the first place. Prices had been distorted by cheap credit and this had led to malinvestments. What was needed was time, to allow the bad effects of excess credit to be worked out of the system "naturally" – without government interference. Hayek was less of an interventionist than even Friedman when it came to the role of government. It was at this juncture in 1974 that Hayek was awarded his Nobel Prize along with Myrdal. Although Hayek and Marx are thought to be polar opposites, a renowned American Marxist, Paul Sweezy, told me that he had gone to the LSE in the 1930s to study under Hayek because he thought "Hayek had the key to capitalism." No wonder, then, that when capitalism was in trouble the ideas of Marx and Hayek were revived together.[4]

Monetarists had advocated control of money supply. Deficits, if there were any, had to be funded by borrowing rather than by printing money. Their theory said this could be done without causing unemployment. The Phillips curve was vertical and the economy, according to the monetarists, just slid down the curve. It did not prove to be so simple and both the UK and the US suffered from severe recessions during the early 1980s. But eventually inflation came down by increasing unemployment – a Phillips curve policy without acknowledging the influence. Western economies abandoned the commitment to full employment and gave priority to controlling inflation. Keynesian economics was dethroned from its perch and began a long embattled life with a new rival claiming the throne.

New Classical Economics

The "new classical economics" had emerged as the rival paradigm by the late 1970s/early 1980s. It superseded monetarism as the new orthodoxy, though it incorporated, rather than rejected, the quantity theory. The idea that Keynesian macroeconomics lacked suitable microeconomic foundations was now generally accepted in academia. Meanwhile the reputation of the Walrasian general equilibrium had been reestablished by the new tools of mathematics which had been developed in the postwar period. Students in the 1960s and 1970s had absorbed the works of Kenneth Arrow and Gerard Debreu, who had given a rigorous foundation to the Walrasian general equilibrium theory. They saw the world as the "Arrow-Debreu economy." There were multiple markets for commodities which all came into equilibrium at the same time for the present and for all instances in the future. There was no need for macroeconomics unless it could be reconciled with the new general equilibrium theory. No Keynes without Walras.

Macro modeling in their view relied on ad hoc rules and shortcuts to justify government actions. They derogatorily referred to it as "hand-waving." They believed government intervention made the problem worse than if it had been left to the market. The sheer unrealism of the Walrasian model was an attraction rather than a hindrance, thanks to its mathematical elegance. Any appeal to "facts" was dismissed as insufficiently rigorous.

Another new influence came in the mid-1960s via the avail-ability of computers large enough to allow statistical work on the movement of stock-market data. Stockbrokers, or "chartists," had always relied on diagrams to forecast the movements of stock prices, but now all stock prices could be stored in a computer disc and analyzed. A significant result emerged. The day-to-day movement (increase or decrease) in any particular stock price was random, that is, unpredictable from past data. The implication was that experts could not outguess the market, which was the result of interaction among thousands of buyers and sellers of stocks. The market was generating "correct" prices and could not be beaten by predictive modeling.

This insight led to the idea of the efficient market hypothesis (EMH). The idea is associated with the Chicago economist Eugene Fama, who did extensive statistical research on stock prices. The result was that the change in a stock price between today and tomorrow could not be predicted from the change over the previous 24 hours or earlier. When he was jointly awarded the Nobel Prize in 2013 with Lars Peter Hansen, also of University of Chicago, and Robert Shiller of Yale University, it was for "empirical analysis of asset prices."

What this implied is that in any market where there are many participants and plentiful information, the buyers and sellers will form their best expectations depending on all the informa-tion available. An important ingredient of this information is their knowledge of how prices are determined by demand and supply. People will form their expectations using all the information added to their knowledge of the "model" of how prices are formed.

One consequence of this notion is that a strategy based on adaptive expectations would not be the best way of operating in the market. When prices are rising, adaptive expectations trail behind, since tomorrow's price is higher than the average of recent past prices, and similarly on the way down. That means the buyer or seller would always be wrong. Rational people ought to learn from their mistakes and not repeat them.

This insight had immediate implications for the Phillips curve. Phillips had modeled the rate of change of money wages as related to unemployment. He did mention prices parenthetically in his article but did not include them in his explicit relationship, largely because, in his main sample of 1861–1913, there had been no discernible inflation or deflation over the 52-year period. Friedman used the logic of adaptive expectations to argue that the Phillips curve would move outward as inflationary expectations were revised upward. But even so the workers could always be behind the actual inflation rate if they used adaptive expectations and inflation was increasing all the while. An inquisitive reader could reasonably ask the question: Why could they not rationally work out that each demand for higher money wages on their part would lead to higher inflation, or why could they not apply the logic of economics to their own situation? Had they done so, they would know that the money wage is neither here nor there. It is the real wage that matters. The level of unemployment would be determined in the labor market where the real wages would determine demand and supply.

Robert Lucas, Friedman's student and colleague at Chicago, asserted convincingly that the Phillips curve had to be vertical at a level of unemployment determined by the microeconomic theory of labor markets. On the issue of money wages and unemployment, economics remained silent since employment and unemployment were determined by real wages, not money wages. Since the days of Keynes's insistence that real wages could not be cut because workers and employers bargained about money wages, economics had come full circle. Real wages were back in the saddle. Neoclassical economics dictated that microeconomic theory was correct and macroeconomics had to dovetail with the microeconomic foundations. Thus the level of unemployment was now determined independently of the rate of rise in money wages, that is, the variable which was of interest in the Phillips curve. The equilibrium natural rate of unemployment was determined outside the space of the Phillips curve. The natural rate was given by the summing of many micro markets and independent of the aggregate money wage. Thus any rate of money wage could be associated with it depending on the rate of inflation. The "true" Phillips curve was thus vertical; with no trade-off between inflation and unemployment (see Figure 7).[5]

Lucas's idea of a vertical Phillips curve implied that inflation was unconnected to the state of the labor market. Inflation was determined by money supply, as Friedman had argued. This was the moment of the birth of new classical economics. All of

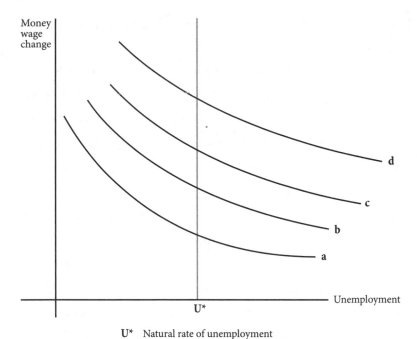

U*   Natural rate of unemployment

Figure 7   Lucas's version of the Phillips curve

Keynes's analysis was challenged and rejected by the new clas-sical economists. The simultaneous arrival of "efficient markets" and "rational expectations" was a crucial step in the change of paradigm in macroeconomics. They reinforced the arguments that not only was there no market failure as Keynes had alleged but that the markets were perfect and the economic agents – workers and employers – knew how to pursue their own inter-ests. An important element in this triumph was the use of familiar words but with a different meaning attached to them. Thus, ef-ficiency was associated with least-cost outcomes in production. Fama used the word in the sense that the market could not be outguessed. But even here the prediction was more limited than later interpretations made it. The forecast one step ahead of the price change of an equity was random in relation to the change in the immediately preceding period. So far so good. But this was meant to rule out any sustained strategy to exploit market movements. The price change might be random from day to day but summing up random numbers can still make a pattern, as Slutsky had shown. But this was denied.

Hayek had argued a very different approach to the market way back in the 1930s. In a lecture to LSE students titled "Economics and Knowledge," he argued that most theories of economics, such as those of Walras, made excessive demands on our knowledge of the world.[6] The consumer in economic theory is assumed to know all prices of all commodities in the present and in possible future scenarios (contingent commodities). Hayek thought this was unrealistic, and indeed, if true, denied the possibilities of free choice since a Planner could know the same and plan all our lives. He argued that the market consisted of pools of local knowledge, which some people had access to, and then it was the division of knowledge parallel to the division of labor which should constitute the subject of economics. Knowledge was decentralized and could not be held in one place or by one agency. The market was a search process and prices signaled where there were opportunities for gain, either in terms of profits or in terms of consumer satisfaction. Hayek's insights were ignored by the new classical economists since they viewed the market to be infallible and omniscient.

The efficient market hypothesis became not just a hypothesis but also a revealed truth. Thus bubbles – the movement of the price of an asset, usually upward – were ruled out on the basis of EMH. There were long debates about the occurrence of bubbles, with new classical economists treating the possibility as absurd and Keynesians taking up bubbles as their disproof of EMH. Robert Shiller, who had argued that the stock market in the 1990s was in a fervor of "irrational exuberance" since stock prices bore little relation to underlying fundamentals, asserted the theoretical and empirical possibility of bubbles.

A similar story can be told about rational expectations (RE). Expectations used to mean your notion of what might be the course of some variable tomorrow or next week. The weather, for example, or the price of tomatoes. Keynes had discussed short-term and long-term expectations in this sense. Lucas defined expectations in the statistical sense as the mean of a distribution of a random variable. Take the well-known bell-shaped distribution. Many random variables, for example the number of cars passing through a traffic light every five minutes in the central business district, will have a bell-shaped distribution. The larger the number of observations of a random variable, the more likely it is to have a bell-shaped or "normal" distribution. Now the mean of the distribution, in ordinary parlance the average of the observations, is called the expectation (or the first moment) of the distribution. In the bell-shaped distribution, it coincides with the peak of the bell. Thus the word expectation means different things in the two contexts.

Those who are supposed to hold rational expectations (i.e. all of us) are assumed to know how the systematic parts of the model work which show how prices are determined. We use that knowledge to generate our prediction. This will be correct except for random influences. We can assume that such random events will adhere to the bell-shaped distribution and its mean/expectation will be zero. Thus the systematic or deterministic prediction based on theory is always correct. Errors have zero expectation. Once the statistical sense was established, the word expectations lost the other meaning in common parlance, at least among academic economists.

The Indeterminacy of Econometric Models

Robert Lucas's next target was the large econometric models which were being deployed to answer issues of policy. These models had become very detailed in terms of the number of variables they attempted to predict and the interconnections among the variables. They were frequently updated and often extended by adding equations and variables. They had become a useful tool for policy analysis and advocacy. The Kennedy-Johnson tax cut of 1963 had been based on the predictions of one such large model. By the early 1970s models had become larger still.

Lucas argued that the models and the estimates they put forward could not be taken to be reflections of individual behavior which the policy-makers could take as constraints.[7] The estimates were a mishmash of behavior and response to policy. In a world of rational agents, any policy pronounced by the government to affect individual decisions could be thwarted by the individuals taking countervailing action. The idea is that rational agents – all of us – are fully conversant with the way an economy works. We may observe that the government is likely to pursue a policy which may harm our self interest. We would then try to frustrate such a policy. Governments have to know this and frame their policies in light of the understanding that citizens are rational agents.

Thus, in a celebrated result, it was argued that if the government tried to spend money by borrowing to reflate the economy, citizens would immediately foresee that such borrowing would have to be repaid out of additional taxes. They would then take countervailing action and save extra, thus nullifying the multiplier effects of the spending. The discounted sum of their savings would exactly match the amount of current spending. This may even require the assumption of infinitely long-lived agents! This was an application of the Ricardian equivalence.

The Klein-type models were descriptions of the way the economy was behaving. They did not give a priori higher status to rational private agents. Each version of the model was often more detailed than the previous one in an attempt better to explain what the policy was trying to do, whether it had succeeded, and what lessons one could learn from previous failures of policies to achieve their aims. Since models got reestimated, they were never pictures of some pristine fixed structure but ongoing summaries of the economic reality.

New classical economics treated such models with the contempt of a purist faced with a worldly sinner. Its adherents believed in their theory as literal truth. In such a world, the government was not in control of the economy. Instead it played a game with its citizens, who could negate the effects of any preannounced policy. Thus policy would have to dovetail with individual preferences to be effective. Individuals maximize the best they can. As they do so, the economy attains an equilibrium. Governments, in trying to influence behavior, can cause harm if they go against individual optimization. The best thing governments can do is to provide a stable framework of rules within which individuals can optimize.

Friedman's critique of Keynes and his advocacy of monetarism and Lucas's systematic construction of a new classical critique undermined the economics profession's faith in Keynesian macroeconomic theory and policy. In the US, economists were said to be from sweetwater departments – from Chicago and Minnesota, where they were new classical – and from saltwater departments – MIT, Harvard and Yale, where they continued to be Keynesians who did not concede the ground totally to the new classical economists. In the teaching of macroeconomics and the modeling of data, the methods and ideas of the new classical economists gained ground. Saltwater economists sought room for policy activism by citing rigidities, which might persist for a short while. Thus, while inflation may be prevalent, not all prices may respond immediately. Some prices may be sticky, that is, the money wage. That could give a small scope for policy activism. Otherwise, all arguments within the economics profession ceased. A Great Moderation prevailed in which most economists had signed up to new classical macroeconomics.

The New Classical Model

By the mid-1980s there had been a truce among the warring faction of economists. In the US, the sweetwater economists of Chicago and Minnesota had won over the saltwater economists of Harvard, MIT and Yale. Keynes had his aggregate demand and supply equations and there are parallel equations in the new classical model.

There is an aggregate supply equation. It shows that aggregate income (Y) deviates from its equilibrium value (Y^* – given from micro behavior) if the price level (P) temporarily deviates from its equilibrium or expected value E (P^*). There is an aggregate demand equation which is derived from the Marshall-Pigou demand for money equation. This says that income (Y) is determined by the amount of real balances (money supply M divided by price level P) multiplied by the velocity ($1/k$) where k is the proportion of income kept by people in liquid terms.

The intersection of aggregate supply and aggregate demand will determine actual income and price level (see Figure 8). Thus if there is excessive money supply, income will exceed its equilibrium value and the price level will be higher than its equilibrium level. We could elaborate this simple scheme by using

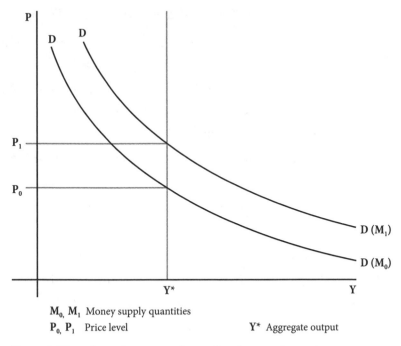

Figure 8 New classical aggregate demand and aggregate supply

M_0, M_1 Money supply quantities

P_0, P_1 Price level $\qquad$ Y^* Aggregate output

Hicks's IS-LM model as an analogy. A new IS curve can be described as saying that aggregate income is determined by the rate of interest and what the government injects into the private economy – public spending plus interest paid on government debt to private citizens.

The new LM equation is very much like the old one. Demand for money is determined by income, price level and the rate of interest.

Thus for the new classical theory, the IS-LM apparatus did not determine the level of income but only the price level and the rate of interest. Income was determined by micro behavior and was given for the purposes of macro outcomes. The new classical macroeconomics thus kept the terminology of Keynesian economics but altered its link of causation. Nominal variables – price level, rate of interest – are determined at the macroeconomic level. Output and by implication employment are determined at the micro level.

The policy implications were then derived. The role of the government was to lay down a medium-term policy framework for spending and borrowing so that private agents could make their consumption plans. The task of the monetary authority was to regulate the money supply so that, given aggregate supply, the price level would not show any sustained inflationary tendency. This was the policy package of the Great Moderation. The anti-inflation stance of the Central Bank entailed making it independent of the fiscal authority. Central Bank independence became a mark of the sincerity of a government. Gordon Brown, on taking office as Chancellor in the New Labour government in 1997, immediately gave the Bank of England autonomy in determining interest rates in pursuit of an inflation target. We had come a long way from the euthanasia of the rentier.

Economists do not do fieldwork as anthropologists do, nor do they, on the whole, experiment in a laboratory as natural scientists do. There is a branch called "experimental economics" but it has not changed the nature of the subject to any great extent. But economists do confront published data. The time series of data on income, consumption, investment and so forth are available on an annual or quarterly basis. Economists model them using statistical techniques, like the models Klein built for the US economy. The new classical economists also modeled the data. They, however, did not forecast or judge the quality of their model by the accuracy of their forecasts. They chose instead to "mimic" the characteristic of their sample. Thus, rather than tracking a particular cycle, they asked if the model generated cycles whose average length matched the average length of the cycle in the sample. Thus the statistical criterion of performance also changed from the previous Keynesian-type models, which had had a more difficult criterion of model performance.

In theory, the equilibrium in Walrasian theory is unique. There could be small deviations around it, as the Lucas model outlined above assumed. There has been no theoretical solution of a Walrasian economy moving in real time, that is, in dynamic terms, thus far. So all we have is the proposition that a static equilibrium can be proved. But the data show constant movement. How to reconcile unique static equilibrium with moving data? Economists from Marx onward regarded cycles as systematic events in market economies or as indicators of market failures. Walrasians rejected both such notions. They attributed the cycles to unsystematic, that is, random, events.

In this endeavor, they were helped by the achievements of Keynesian policies in the postwar years. There had been steady growth of income in the post–1945 period and recessions had been mild. Thus the data on income fitted a strong trend of steady growth with some fluctuations around it. The negative deviations from the trend never lasted long before reversing themselves, and neither did the positive ones. Thus the success of Keynesian macro policies undermined the Keynesian analysis that cycles were evidence of market failures. They could be seen as accidents, random events.

The idea was always there that all the data are subject to random errors due to measurement errors, omission of less significant variables and pure random chance. But apart from those factors, the new classical economists posited that there were two further "shocks." There are technological shocks which move the aggregate supply up or down, and there are preference shocks which move consumption up or down. The details of these shocks were never specified since they were just devices to accommodate movements in the data. But these shocks made the models *dynamic* and *stochastic*. As they were derived from general equilibrium theory in any case, we had the birth of dynamic stochastic general equilibrium (DSGE) models. These were more elaborate than the new classical three equations scheme presented above, but the elaboration did not change the structure of the argument. These DSGE models are now ubiquitous in Treasury, Central Bank and other policy-making agencies.[8] They have displaced the older Keynesian models of the Klein-Goldberger type.

The DSGE models claim consistency of the macro models with the microeconomic theory. Yet they do so by finessing the aggregation problem which I have discussed above. The real challenge is to have many different consumers and aggregate their preferences into one single macro equation. A typical DSGE model tackles the micro–macro mapping by assuming a single consumer/producer or infinitely many but identical consumers/ producers. Thus the consumption function is derived from the utility functions of individuals who maximize utility defined in terms of total consumption, labor/leisure and real money balances, subject to a constraint that includes current income plus earning from capital stock owned, that is, permanent income. Different types of capital items – houses or equities – are not distinguished. Each individual is meant to supply one unit of labor in terms of which he or she has a monopoly and can be a price setter. All individuals' labor supply can be aggregated as they have an identical utility function. One firm or many identical firms produce the final good using an identical production function.

Thus the micro foundations are just that of a single-person economy facing a single firm (being presumably the only worker). There are no banks, stockbrokers, mortgage lenders. There are bonds but no equities. An earlier generation of Keynesian economists, especially Lawrence Klein in his 1950 Cowles Foundation monograph *Economic Fluctuations in the United States, 1921–1941,* had tried genuinely to work out the aggregation issue, though with only partial success. The DSGE models are toy constructions based on evading the issue of a macro–micro match.

The presence of random shocks helps reproduce mild cyclical fluctuations according to the same idea as Slutsky had put forward. Paradoxically, the success of Keynesian policies helped the success of the DSGE models. The rocking horse did not need to rock for long. What they could not predict was the sharp break and fall in the income trend that occurred in 2008. But to touch on that now would be to get ahead of our story.

The advent of monetarist policies and right-of-center political leaders in the developed countries led to many financial revolutions. One was the removal of the restrictions on capital movements which had been instituted at Bretton Woods. Another was called the Big Bang; among other things, it opened the London Stock Exchange up to international competition and moved it away from its cozy club atmosphere. American stock markets had already been competitive and innovative. The US had liberalized in the early 1970s. The year 1973 witnessed the Chicago Board of Trade open the Chicago Options Exchange to allow centralized trading in options on listed stocks. Options are contingent claims on equities. They were bets that committed an option holder to buy or sell an option by a certain date. The potential buyer was said to have a long position and the seller a short position. The pricing of options became a subject of study. In 1973, the very same year in which option trading became more regular, two economists, Fisher Black and Myron Scholes, presented an analysis which put options in a broader class of contingent assets the price of which could be determined by sophisticated probability analysis.[9] (Fisher Black left his job at MIT to join Solomon Brothers. When asked what persuaded him, he replied, "They added a zero to my salary.")

Forward and futures trading had always existed. But in forward trading, the commitment to buy is unconditional. The trader usually hopes to be able to sell the contract on to someone else before the due date arrives and pocket the profit. Keynes, who used to dabble in such activities, once had the prospect of receiving a hefty delivery of wheat and went about measuring King's College Chapel to see if it could accommodate the large amount.

An option allows the holder not to exercise it if the price is not right. Thus options can never have negative value, while forward contracts can. But then many more such assets can be invented whose value is derivative upon the value of another underlying asset. I can bet on the value of the Dow-Jones index as it would be at some future date. Derivatives were built around values of mortgage contracts, likely revenues of ski resorts – betting on the likelihood of snowfall – and various other ingenious schemes for betting money. They were ways for the holder of an asset to pass on the risks to other people. Financial markets were about to explode with opportunities for trading and betting.

Economists have a theory for the valuation of assets that yield a stream of returns. Keynes, in his theory of liquidity preference, compared people's preference for cash relative to consols, which are bonds with a perpetual yield. The basic idea developed that in buying financial (and by extension real) assets, people weigh up the return versus the risk. Cash carries no risk and yields no return. From then on, one can rank assets by return as measured by the average yield and risk as measured by the variance of the return. The risk–return "frontier" is like a constraint. Each investor can then define his or her preference between risk and return, as with consumer utility functions. To maximize the preference we need the tangent of the preference function with the risk–return frontier, that is, the highest level of return consistent with the risk preference of the consumer. This gives us a theory of portfolio selection for investors, who may choose between cash, bonds, equities and other riskier assets. The growth of knowledge in portfolio selection gave a fillip to the use of mathematical methods. With high-speed computers, it became possible to model portfolio strategies and then allow computers to engage in program trading, that is, automatically buying and selling when the price of an asset reached a certain level. As computers became faster, the trading was done in high frequency, in seconds rather than minutes or hours. Stock markets became virtual instead of trading floors with shouting dealers. Given telephonic connections, markets could have global participants.

Nothing in these developments changed the pursuit of economists in framing their macro models. They carried on with one asset – bonds – and money as if the financial markets would all impinge on the economy via a single interest rate. It seemed to them that once they had explained portfolio choice, the technological developments in the number of assets and the speed with which they could be bought and sold had no relevance for macroeconomics.

In principle, the theory of portfolio selection and the availability of sophisticated financial services are for everyone. But the distribution of wealth in every society is even more unequal than that of income. In the US in 2010, the bottom 90 percent owned under 15 percent of all wealth and the top 10 percent the rest. As you go higher up within the top 10 percent the distribution gets even more shockingly uneven, with the top 1 percent owning 35 percent. Most people never own an equity or a bond. So much of the theory benefits the wealthier people. At most, it is houses where ownership is the widest, but even then it seldom applies to the majority of the population except in the richest countries. But modern economics does not believe such distinctions matter. All individuals are rational maximizing individuals with income and wealth available as constraints on their optimizing behavior.

PART THREE

Chapter Six

THE NEW GLOBALIZATION

We have come some distance on our journey from the earliest days of speculations about money and the economy to some tenacious disputes among academic economists about the nature of the subject and the validity of rival approaches. Yet that is just the prologue. We now need to get down to the real challenge of explaining what happened in the global economy which ended in the Great Recession. Even more important we need to ask why it happened. This will be the test of our alternative approach to the understanding of the economy.

One of the greatest problems in the social sciences, if not in all life, is to be able to separate causation from simple correlation or coincidence. David Hume was skeptical of any demonstration of causality. All one could say, according to him, was that **a** happened before **b** did but not that **a** *caused* **b**. But with the proliferation of statistical methods, data, models and computers, it is tempting to derive causal conclusions from data. One such conclusion was derived from the events that took place in the 1990s and 2000s. This was that the Great Moderation had finally solved the problem of boom and bust. The prospect was of perpetual high employment and low inflation with sustained income growth. Mervyn (now Lord) King, while he was Governor of the Bank of England, described the future as one of non-inflationary continuous expansion (NICE).

The Long Boom

The background to these happy thoughts had been the benevolent economic climate in the developed countries for the previous decade or so.[1] Once again, political events shaped the economic context. In 1989, the Berlin Wall was smashed by demonstrators. Soon after, the Soviet Union disintegrated and the Eastern European nations abandoned Soviet-style rule and became open democratic economies able to pursue free market policies. The success was not only an ideological one. It had profound economic implications. At a stroke, several markets were added to global trade, leading to expanded profit-making opportunities for businessmen and financial traders alike. The course of capitalism, which had been disturbed during World War I by the Bolshevik Revolution and further distorted by the Cold War after the settlement of 1945 and the descent of the Iron Curtain across Eastern Europe, resumed its almost universal coverage of the world.

Capitalism, as Marx and Engels had pointed out way back in 1848, was a global mode of production. Now globalization was on everyone's minds again. This wasn't the first episode of globalization, as we've seen; the world was globalized earlier, most recently in the second half of the nineteenth century. World War I had disrupted this process. The world became divided into capitalism and socialism. After World War II it was seen as being comprised of three worlds: the First World, the developed capitalist countries; the Second World, the Soviet Union and its socialist satellites; and the Third World, the developing countries which pursued a path midway between capitalism and socialism. Globalization resumed its course from 1991 onward. Financial markets were now able to buy and sell financial assets practically around the world with the exception of the highly restrictive regimes of North Korea and Cuba. Even China was beginning to welcome foreign direct investment, though not yet portfolio investment. India was also open to foreign capital and embarked upon a liberal trade regime. International trade had been slowly liberalizing under the General Agreement on Tariffs and Trade. But, during the Uruguay Round – the eighth round of multinational trade negotiations – the developing countries put forth their own demands. Championed mainly by the newly industrialized countries (NICs), they demanded better access to Western markets for their manufactures, including symmetrical treatment with developed countries. To appreciate the revolutionary nature of this development, one has to recall that as recently as in 1975 the United Nations Industrial Development

Organization (UNIDO) had declared at its conference in Lima, Peru an ambitious target to have the share of the emerging economies in manufacturing exports at 25 percent by the year 2000. The data showed that NICs were already marching past this goal. They were demanding markets for their products and freer trade. In response, the World Trade Organization (WTO) was established in 1994 and developing countries joined it with a commitment to cut tariffs and quotas and to liberalize trade.

As trade grew, so did capital flows from the developed to the developing countries, and sometimes in the reverse direction as well. Foreign aid – government to government assistance – became a less significant part of such international flows. China and India became major recipients of private capital flows, along with the nations of Southeast Asia and Latin America. Countries abandoned their *dirigiste* policies and adopted liberal ones. The market was on the march around the world.

One major consequence of the dominance of free market ideology was the privatization of previously nationalized industries. This process had started in the UK where industries nationalized during the postwar Attlee governments of 1945–51 were denationalized by the Thatcher governments of 1979–87. Soon other countries followed the British lead. This move toward privatization of industries in most cases increased their efficiency and improved their profitability. But there was also pressure on mutually owned institutions – the building societies in the UK, for example – to become mainstream profit-making companies, whose equities could be held by anyone. Demutualization proceeded apace during the 1980s and 1990s.

Through the course of the 1990s there was a huge push to deregulate banking in the US. The Glass–Steagall Act passed during the New Deal had regulated the commercial banks which took retail deposits about the sort of investment activities they could engage in. The new complaint of the US banks was that Glass-Steagall restricted competition. Retail deposit-taking is profitable, not so much for itself but because it can provide a large source of idle funds for a bank to invest on its own account and make profits. Investment banks could make such profits. The demand was for retail deposit-taking banks to be allowed to combine with investment banks. To this effect, certain provisions of the Glass-Steagall Act were repealed. Now banks were able to merge the different activities and became much larger.

Most developed countries had some regulatory institutions for financial and commodity markets. But the pace of innovation in the financial markets was fast. There was also the ideological pressure to leave markets alone as they were held to be working perfectly based on the efficient market hypothesis and rational expectations. Regulators themselves believed in these truths, as Alan Greenspan later testified when the crisis had hit. Thus regulatory systems failed en masse to either foresee or give effective forewarning about the coming crisis.

There was also the growth of consumer credit as a result of companies issuing debit and credit cards. Credit cards were first introduced to provide financial security to individuals traveling for business purposes. American banks did not have extensive branches across the country as European banks did. A person away from their home state had to carry cash or travelers' checks. Now a debit or credit card allowed people to have access to purchasing power wherever they were. But soon these cards proliferated and the credit standards – as to the eligibility of who could get them – were lowered to the point that having a credit card became almost universal. Consumers were now able to get into debt much more easily, and indeed more carelessly, than before. Card-issuing companies gave special offers of zero interest charges for the first six months to entice new customers. It was a profitable business.

The prosperity of the postwar years had made the purchase of consumer durables feasible for middle-income families. But there was one more frontier to reach. This was home ownership. Across developed countries, governments adopted policies that eased the process of obtaining mortgages. Often they used positive measures to encourage home ownership. The UK government for many years allowed tax deduction for interest paid on mortgages. Banks or more specialized institutions such as building societies lent money for house buying by facilitating mortgages. The Clinton Administration facilitated the granting of mortgages to households who would otherwise not qualify for loans on orthodox banking criteria of sound lending. This was seen as a positive redistributive measure to spread wealth to poorer households. Housing finance became an important part of bank lending, and a house bought on mortgage an important part of the household portfolio.

The spread of home ownership became a central policy plank for democratic governments of Western economies. The earlier emphasis was on public housing, which was made available to workers as tenants at affordable subsidized rents. Now the idea was that people should own and not rent homes. But they owned their homes with mortgages. The monthly mortgage payments were akin to rents but they gave some equity in the home to the borrower. This gave the illusion of ownership, while in fact the actual owner was the lender until the mortgage was paid off or relinquished.

Durable goods are *stocks* which yield a *flow* of services. A refrigerator is a stock which yields cooling services over its life-time. But it depreciates in value and has to be kept in repair by spending money on its upkeep. But over time the value of the refrigerator deteriorates. A new car, once bought, cannot be resold at the same price, but would face a discount. However, there came to be a belief that houses can only appreciate in their value. Thus families began to believe that buying a house on mortgage was to invest in an appreciating asset. Governments and lenders encouraged such beliefs and soon societies came to assume that the only form in which they needed to save and invest was houses.

House price bubbles came to be a frequent phenomenon in the postwar years. Land being in fixed supply, a Ricardian prediction would be a rise in value of land relative to other commodities. House prices rose because the value of the land on which they stood was rising. Inflation had become a fact of life during the postwar years from the mid-1960s onward till the 1990s, before Central Banks and governments began to adopt inflation targets to keep it under control. House prices were thus rising along with all prices, but also relatively more because of land scarcity. Yet the expectation of a perpetual rise in house prices was to prove a fatal weakness in advanced economies. It was predicated upon inflation being a permanent fact of life.

The Asian Crisis of 1997

Elsewhere, the search for stability in foreign exchange markets continued as more and more countries began to experience significant trade and capital movements.[2] This was a new development for most of them, because they had previously run highly protected and sheltered economies. The newly industrialized countries of Asia became large recipients of foreign capital. This threatened to increase the value of their currency relative to their competitor countries. To avoid this possibility, some had defensively pegged their currency to the US dollar. Thailand was one such country where the local currency – the baht – was pegged to the dollar. Investors from abroad took this to mean that there was no exchange rate risk if they bought assets in Thailand. There was boom in real estate prices as capital poured in. But in standard Wicksellian fashion, doubts set in as inflationary pressures mounted and the Central Bank was expected to curb inflation.

This was the point at which foreign investors began to liquidate their investments. Two things happened. The bubble burst, and so what they were getting out was lower than the recent market price. But more important, the Central Bank of Thailand did not have the dollar reserves to be able to convert baht investments into dollars for the sellers. The baht went off the peg and crashed on the forex market. The contagion of this shock spread to otherwise healthy economies such as Malaysia, South Korea and Indonesia. They were open economies relying on exports and receiving large capital inflows. They had been hailed just a decade previously as Asian Tigers. Now they were caught in a global storm. They had insufficient reserves to facilitate withdrawals of large amounts of foreign capital. There was drastic depreciation in the currencies of all the major Asian countries that had opened up their capital markets. The Asian crisis was a deeply humiliating experience for these countries, which had to rush to the IMF for emergency help.

There had been crises before. During the 1980s many developing countries experienced debt, having borrowed money in the 1970s when the rate of interest was low. When monetary policy became anti-inflationary in the developed countries, interest rates shot up and debts could not be serviced. This inaugurated the decade of misery for the developing countries which began with the Mexican debt crisis and lasted through the 1980s. It was eventually resolved by creditors accepting cancellation of debt and the debtor countries selling some of their natural resources in lieu of repayment of the principal.

Mexico was thought to have restored financial prudence and fixed its exchange rates after it had recovered from its debt problem. But in 1994, Mexico was hit by the Mexican peso crisis. Investors from across the world had bought Mexican bonds – the *tesebonos*. But political turmoil in the Chiapas region led to a panicked withdrawal of capital and a collapse of the peso. The IMF arranged a large loan to help Mexico overcome the shock of the sudden collapse of the currency. This remained a local issue and did not spread beyond Mexico to the US. That, after all, was why the IMF made one of the largest loans it had ever made. Mexico is nearer to the US than Thailand is.

The Asian crisis was different. It came to countries which by all accounts had performed an economic miracle, and its contagion spread across most of Asia. The crisis threatened to spread to Russia and Brazil. But the US Federal Reserve acted quickly and decisively, much as the Bank of England used to, by cutting interest rates and injecting a lot of liquidity into the global banking system.

There was a fascinating episode which should have been instructive for economists and active traders. During the brief interval when Russian bonds were falling in price, an American investment company – Long-Term Capital Management – whose directors included Nobel Prize winning economists, went bust.[3] The basic strategy of the company was based on the assumption that if the interest rate differential widened between a US bond and a foreign bond, one should invest in the foreign bond as sooner or later the rates would converge. The foreign bond would appreciate in price as its yield declined to catch up with the US yield. During the brief crisis of 1998, interest rates widened rather than narrowed. The financial markets did not converge toward an equilibrium as theory had predicted but diverged. This was what was later called a Black Swan event – a statistical rarity. The firm was heavily leveraged and could not meet the payments required to make up the loss. It had to be rescued by a consortium of banks and investment firms on Wall Street under the guidance of the Federal Reserve Bank of New York.

By pumping liquidity into the markets, the Federal Reserve prevented the Russian crisis from spreading to Western countries. The Asian countries learned a pivotal lesson. If domestic firms, banks or manufacturers are about to go bust, they can be rescued through the printing of currency. But their Central Banks or governments could not print dollars and that is what the punters were demanding. The global financial powers were not going to come to the rescue of remote Asian economies unless they thought the crisis might affect them at home.

The policy implications for Asian countries affected by the crisis and others such as China and India which had never let capital come in freely were clear: do not rely on the IMF or anyone else for help. Be self-reliant as far as the needs of foreign exchange reserves are concerned. The repercussions were to affect the dynamics of globalization in the decade to come. These countries began to export aggressively and pile up large reserves of foreign exchange. In a way, this was a return to the mercantilist policy; depriving their citizens of cheap imports which they could have bought with their export earnings. But they chose instead to be risk averse and piled up reserves. And since they needed to earn a modicum of return on these reserves, they put them in the US Treasury securities (T bills), which provided the most liquid form of investment available internationally.

The proliferation of financial crises during the 1980s and 1990s were all in the periphery, that is, the developing countries, and not at the core, in the developed or metropolitan economies. Financial crises were thus viewed as a result of weak economic governance or the pursuit of policies which were not market-friendly, or insufficiently so. Crises happened over there, not at home; or so the economists of the developed world, or those working at the IMF, believed.

The Rise and Collapse of the Great Moderation

The decade following the Asian crash was a continuous boom period for the developed countries. Even the developing economies, previously victims of crises and often dismissed as problems, now became known as emerging economies as they benefited from continuous growth of the developed economies and the benevolent effects of the WTO. Jim O'Neill of Goldman Sachs coined the acronym BRIC to represent Brazil, Russia, India and China as a group of four high-growth economies. Later, South Africa was added to the list to make it BRICS. The creation of the acronym signified the shifting center of global economic activity eastward and southward. China had notched up double-digit GDP growth for nearly 20 years by then and had emerged as a potential giant soon to rival Japan and the US in size of total GDP. India had also woken up from its four decades of slow, so-called "Hindu rate of growth" and was growing at high single-digit rates. These were the two economies with low to moderate per capita income but a billion plus in population each. Brazil and Russia were economies rich in land and minerals that were beginning to realize their potential. But there were other economies – Indonesia, Malaysia, South Korea – that were not far behind in the vigor of their GDP growth.

Three important things happened the significance of which both singly and jointly was not recognized by economists in academia or in policy-making circles. Firstly, the entry of China and other Asian countries in the global economy as exporters of manufacturing goods had shifted the supply curve of manufactures to the right. It had made manufactures permanently cheaper than they used to be. During the 1960s and 1970s, inflation in developed countries was often blamed on the increase in prices of manufactured goods. This inflationary tendency was attributed by the Keynesians to imperfections in competition or wage rigidity. Now, with the source of manufacturing goods having shifted to the developing economies, manufacturing prices were removed as a likely source of inflation. Inflation had become permanently lower in the developed economies, but this was attributed to the Great Moderation or astute Central Bank policy rather than the real conditions of manufacturing supply.

Secondly, at the same time as inflation moved to a lower level, the Asian countries which had amassed large forex reserves deposited them in US T bill markets. This was very similar to what the oil-exporting nations had done during the 1970s after the oil shock. So, thirdly, this made the supply of cheap credit possible by driving down the yields on T bills. During the 1970s it was the poorer nations which had borrowed excessively. Now it was the turn of the richer nations. Cheap credit thus continued for a second decade for the developed countries, since global financial markets could transmit cheap credit from the US outward. This combination of easy credit and low inflation was unique and was attributed to the superior understanding economists had acquired of how markets worked. It was in fact the consequence of globalization. A confident belief began to be held by economists that any adverse effects of globalization such as those felt by the Asian economies were more a function of their lack of understanding of monetary theory and policy than any problem with the global economy. The developed economies had conquered the problem of "boom and bust," as Gordon Brown, the Chancellor of the Exchequer in the UK, asserted. Alas, the fundamentals of economic life had not changed.

In a world of low interest rates, the search for high yields intensified. A variety of agents grew up promising large wealth-holders higher than the widely available yields. Businesses such as hedge funds, private equity firms and "special vehicles," which could treat money in imaginative ways to assure better than average returns, proliferated. They could borrow from banks on the strength of their collateral, and indeed behaved like shadow banks. Financial innovations also began to explode. The original idea of Black and Scholes on pricing options was extended to more sophisticated instruments using the calculation of risk based on statistical mathematics (stochastic calculus), allowing for the creation of new assets even when the buyers (and often even the sellers) could not quite grasp the principles underlying such assets. University finance departments attracted math and science graduates and the legend grew of "rocket scientists" working in brokerage firms inventing new assets.

Perhaps the simplest idea in spreading risk is to combine two assets whose prices move in opposite directions. In technical terms, they have a negative covariance. Portfolios that included a larger number of such assets had lower average risk. One innovation was to combine mortgages into an equity bundle. Banks or other mortgage lenders could take, say, 1,000 mortgages they had issued of a million dollars each and splice up the billion-dollar bundle into 10,000 shares of 100,000 dollars each. Each equity is a combination of the thousand mortgages that underlie the equity bundle. This was called the securitization of mortgages. Buyers of such equities felt reassured that they had diversified their risk. This was doubly so if a rating agency could rate it as triple A, which many rating agencies promptly did.

Cheap credit abounded but there were few avenues available for productive investments. At the end of the 1990s a big rally in the stock markets, chastised for its "irrational exuberance" by Alan Greenspan, came to an end when the dot.com boom collapsed.

The IT innovations and their follow-ups had been like a Schumpeterian innovation cycle; the collapse of the dot.com boom signaled its coming to an end. While waiting for the next innovation, money went into the mortgage market. The US government continued to encourage the extending of mortgage loans to families who would previously not have got such loans. Its agencies Fannie Mae and Freddie Mac were there to underwrite mortgages and were enthusiastically doing so. Thus arose the subprime mortgage boom. The borrowers often had insufficient income to service the mortgage but could always borrow extra to do so in the hope that eventually the house price would rise and valorize their debts. The banks issued mortgages, spliced them up into equities and sold them to each other as well as to other investors. Even foreign investors such as German banks got into the act as these were supposed to be triple A securities which were guaranteed by the US government (not technically so, but de facto).

Interest rates in the US had averages at around 6 percent between 1971 and 2001. By 2005 they had come down to nearly 1 percent, falling steadily from above 5 percent in 2000. Raghuram Rajan, who was Chief Economist of the IMF and a professor at Chicago, did warn in 2005 that there were fault lines in the global financial architecture which financial innovations might expose. But he was dismissed as a "Luddite."

This was an amazing situation, with low inflation, low interest rates and plenty of credit. But then another aspect of globalization impinged on the world economy. GDP growth accelerated in China and this put pressure on raw material prices, especially oil prices. The Fed saw signs of impending inflation and US interest rates went up to 5 percent by 2007.

This was the classic Wicksellian situation. The market rate of interest had been so low that investments with even a modest rate of return – a low natural rate – had become profitable to invest in. But what was profitable at 1 percent could not be so at 5 percent. The boom collapsed. Even before that moment arrived, there had been signs that perhaps the bubble was about to burst. In a famous line, Chuck Prince, who was CEO of Citibank, was quoted as saying "I have to keep dancing till the music stops," implying that while he was aware he was taking on too much risk, he had to since his competitors were also doing so. His bank's profits depended on his frenzied activity. Keynes had anticipated this situation in his *General Theory*:

> In one of the greatest investment markets in the world, namely, New York, the influence of speculation . . . is enormous. . . . It is rare, one is told, for an American to invest, as many Englishmen still do, "for income"; and he will not readily purchase an investment except in the hope of capital appreciation. This is only another way of saying that, when he purchases an investment, the American is attaching his hopes, not so much to its prospective yield, as to a favourable change in the conventional basis of valuation, i.e. that he is, in the above sense, a speculator. Speculators may do no harm as bubbles on a steady stream of enterprise. But the position is serious when enterprise becomes the bubble on a

whirlpool of speculation. When the capital development of a country becomes a by-product of the activities of a casino, the job is likely to be ill-done. The measure of success attained by Wall Street, regarded as an institution of which the proper social purpose is to direct new investment into the most profitable channels in terms of future yield, cannot be claimed as one of the outstanding triumphs of *laissez-faire* capitalism – which is not surprising, if I am right in thinking that the best brains of Wall Street have been in fact directed towards a different object.[4]

The crash when it came first hit the banks.[5] They had overextended their lending and bought each other's dubious packages of securitized mortgages and other derivative products. It was like the children's game of Pass the Parcel. When the music stopped, each was left holding a parcel and did not know what the parcel contained. The risks, instead of being diversified, multiplied through interconnections. Interbank lending seized up.

When a company goes bankrupt, one is bound to ask: Did the efficient market or the participants with rational expectations foresee this? How can equity in Bear Stearns be worth $110 one day and be sold soon after for $10? Is it the case that far from all information being public as the efficient market hypothesis assumes, accounting can hide problems? On the eve of its bankruptcy, three different potential purchasers were trying to read the accounts of Lehman Brothers and were none the wiser as to its asset/liabilities situation. These were specialists. How could an ordinary investor know what the specialist with access to books could not find out?

If the market always gets it right, as the investors and the regulators had been told, then why were people surprised by the sudden collapse in equity prices and capital values of previously profitable firms? Alan Greenspan, as Chairman of the Federal Reserve from 1987 to 2006, had presided over the financial revolution, globalization and the long boom. He believed in free markets and had accepted the theories emanating from the Chicago School of economics. Once the boom collapsed, he recanted. In his testimony to a committee of the US House of Representatives, he explained what happened. The exposition is illuminating:

It was the failure to properly price such risky assets [mortgage backed securities and collateral debt obligations] that precipitated the crisis. In recent decades, a vast risk management and pricing system has evolved, combining the best insights of mathematicians and finance experts, supported by major advances in computer and communications technology. A Nobel Prize was awarded for the discovery of the pricing model that underpins much of the advance in derivative markets. This modern risk management paradigm held sway for decades. The whole intellectual edifice, however, collapsed in the summer of last year because the data inputted into the risk management models generally covered only the past two decades, a period of euphoria. Had instead the models been fitted more appropriately to historic periods of stress, capital requirements would have been much higher and the financial world would be in far better shape today, in my judgment.[6]

In essence, the mathematical technique were hiding a short-sighted outlook. The data used were taken from the two decades of steady growth, cheap money and rising markets. It was then treated as a reflection of the true underlying reality. The future was predicted to be like the recent past. Once the data were incorporated into a model the result given was that the current circumstances would last forever. The statistical tools used, as I'll show in the following chapter, were not sophisticated; they were in fact quite simple. Regulatory institutions were also caught in the same theoretical logic of market efficiency and rational expectations.

A report by the UK Financial Services Authority authored by its CEO Lord Adair Turner gives a revealing insight into how regulatory institutions suffered from an "ideological capture" by the market participants. The report summarized five propositions which had implications for the regulatory approach that the FSA had followed:

1 Market prices are a good indication of rationally evaluated economic value.
2 The development of securitized credit, since based on the creation of new and more liquid markets, has improved both allocative efficiency and financial stability.

3 The risk characteristics of financial markets can be inferred from mathematical analyses, delivering robust quantitative measures of trading risk.

4 Market discipline can be used as an effective tool in constraining harmful risk-taking.

5 Financial innovation can be assumed to be beneficial since market competition would winnow out any innovations which did not deliver value-added.[7]

The regulators were thus incapable of thinking outside and away from the box in which the received theory had put them. If the model admits no possibility of failure of prediction, and the regulator accepts the model's assumptions, the results are that both the poacher and the gamekeeper will lose. The malaise once again is in the theory not in the real world.

Can Capital Be Fairly Valued?

Valuation of capital is taken by neoclassical economics to be a simple straightforward issue. The value of a capital asset is the discounted sum of its future expected earnings. Formulae exist to calculate it mathematically. But if a capital asset worth a thousand dollars today is worth one dollar the next day, then either the stream of earnings is dubious, or our expectations are overly optimistic, or we are applying the wrong discount rate. Of course, even if everything was fine this calculation applies to an equity regularly traded on an active deep market. When we come to residential or commercial property, either finished or even trickier under construction, it would be a brave economist who could tell you how such a capital asset is valued. Secondhand capital goods are notoriously hard to value as they are often single items for which the markets are quite thin. Theories of efficient markets are constructed for easily tradable equities, preferably on the New York Stock Exchange. Outside that narrow confine, even the best theory is clueless.

During the 1960s, an arcane debate broke out between the economists of Cambridge, England and those of Cambridge, Massachusetts (mainly MIT). It was called the measurement of capital debate. It was fought across learned journals and in mathematically abstruse articles. The English were questioning the validity of the neoclassical theory of factor rewards, that is, the idea that labor gets its marginal product and capital its own marginal product in an aggregate production function context. The details of the debate need not detain us. But one idea advanced in the Cambridge, England critique was that such valuations can be made only by assuming equilibrium. They cannot be used to analyze how an economy will get to an equilibrium if disturbed from it. Out of equilibrium, there are no hard and fast rules for valuing capital.

In some sense this is what happened in the crisis. Capital values plummeted, while the productive equipment, the human capital and the relevant prices such as interest rates had not changed to anything like the same extent. One could say that expectations had changed. But then that is like a device which will explain just about anything.

Recession and the Prospect of Recovery

The latest recession has been characterized by certain features that set it apart from previous recessions. The US and the UK, as well as many of the eurozone countries, have a high debt to GDP ratio, as well as large current budget deficits. Households have also been highly indebted, with their principal asset – houses – depreciating in value and thus facing negative equity. Banks required recapitalization in the US and the UK. It looks likely that this experience will be repeated in the eurozone countries. There are also global imbalances at play, with many "emerging" economies having large surplus foreign exchange reserves and the developed countries, especially the US, indebted to them.

The lackluster recovery has become a contentious issue, with some arguing that its fragility is a result of the cautious fiscal response by governments wedded to cutting budget deficits rather than boosting fiscal spending. The UK economy is now committed to eliminating the budget deficit completely by 2018–19. It is currently estimated to be at 6 per cent of GDP. The US was given a large fiscal boost of around $800 billion in 2009, but even after two years it had failed to speed up the recovery. The Keynesian troops have been arguing the case for a stronger fiscal response. Their mantra – focus on spending the economy out of recession now and worry about the debt deficit issues later on.[8]

But in reality this remedy would only work if the recession were a Keynesian one to begin with. A recession of the Keynesian type would typically arise from a collapse of effective demand due to oversaving. But the years preceding the recession were characterized by households undersaving rather than over-saving, borrowing beyond their capacity to repay rather than hoarding or refraining from consumption. Governments in most developed economies were also borrowing even at the peak of the cycle, where Keynes's advice would have been to achieve a surplus on the budget and repay the debt.

The income growth trend achieved during the long boom of 1992–2007 would not have been sustainable without borrowing. The household debt to income ratio rose, as did the national debt to GDP ratio across developed countries. Inevitably debts have to be repaid at some stage and that requires savings. It is the households' and the governments' desire to reduce the debt burden which has resulted in a slow recovery.

Keynesians are in favor of disregarding the existing burden and borrowing to stimulate growth, which in their view would cure the disease. But governments borrowed during the boom and have continued to do so since the collapse of the boom. The borrowing during the upswing should have led to extra growth and revenue, which would then have serviced the debt. Nothing of the sort seems to have happened. Deficits high during the upswing rose during the recession, as would be expected. The cumulative burden of deficits incurred in good times added to those required in bad times means that the debt burden is rising, not falling.

More borrowing would need to be shown to be a cure rather than a worsening of the problem. In a closed economy, as Keynes argued, any increase in the savings rate may lead to a drop in income. But in an open economy within a global capital market, repayment of debts may attract capital from abroad as the credit rating of the country improves. The recession was caused by overspending by governments and households thanks to cheap credit fueled by the global imbalances. It is the sort of recession predicted by Hayek in his work during the 1930s.

It is widely agreed by governments across OECD countries that the path of fiscal expansion is closed off. Such unanimity is rare. The answer instead has been to allow Central Banks to buy bonds aggressively to pump money into the system. This policy originates from Milton Friedman and Anna Schwartz's *Monetary History of the United States*.[9] They blamed the severity of the Great Depression on the Fed's policy of restricting the money supply. Ben Bernanke, the Fed Chairman who studied the Great Depression as his Ph.D. topic, took the lesson to heart. The policy of quantitative easing has been the norm for five years in the US and the UK. Japan has also joined the ranks. The European Central Bank is also contemplating adopting this strategy as the rate of inflation has fallen below 1 percent in the eurozone area.

Keynes was skeptical about the efficacy of monetary policy to stimulate the economy out of depression. But the British recovery during the mid-1930s was based on monetary policy rather than fiscal policy. Neville Chamberlain, the then Chancellor of the Exchequer, cut Bank Rate to 2 percent and reduced the debt servicing burden by refinancing the debt at 3.5 percent rather than 5 percent, as we saw above. The British had also abandoned the Gold Standard and hence devalued their currency. It was these monetary policy moves which aided the recovery. A recovery that was faster in the UK than in the US. This historical experience was somewhat ignored by the postwar fashion of simplifying Keynes's message, leading to the rigid conclusion drawn by the earlier generation of Keynesians that monetary policy was ineffective in engineering a recovery. The adage was: "You cannot push on a string."

Yet the injection of a large quantity of liquidity has not revived the economies of the US and UK. The best you can say is that the recession was not deepened thanks to the regime of low interest rates. What is also surprising is that the enormous amount of money injected into the economy has not caused inflation, as was the doctrine of the monetarists during the 1970s. But then the monetarists also had a closed economy model and the world has become open and globalized. In fact, much of the money has gone abroad in search of higher yields via hedge funds and private equity firms. The emerging economies have been experiencing sustained inflows of capital, which have led to an appreciation of their exchange rate. During the summer of 2013, when rumors were spreading that the Fed might reverse the quantitative easing policy and begin tapering, there was a sharp increase in the depreciation of the currencies of emerging economies, leading to increased volatility in the equity markets.

The argument that the recession would have been much worse had there not been a sustained policy of keeping interest rates low is a counterfactual which is difficult to disprove. The low interest rates which have persisted have given households room to deleverage slowly rather than being forced into mortgage foreclosures, as has happened in earlier recessions. This may have eased the pain of holding negative equity. Many firms – Zombie firms, as they are called – have avoided bankruptcy thanks to the historically low interest rates. But then, at the same time, it has also postponed the required adjustment to correct the core problem of too much debt. This leads to the problem of a *stock disequilibrium*. Let me explain.

If I borrow, my borrowing is a *flow* which adds to my *stock* of debt. Budget deficit is a flow while public debt is a stock. While the deficit is not eliminated, the stock of debt goes on rising. What I can afford by way of the flow of borrowing and the stock of debt would depend on the flow of income I have and the stock of assets (my house) that I possess. If I have a high income and plenty of assets I can borrow to the hilt because my stock/flow relation will be in equilibrium, that is, affordable. My stocks of assets and liabilities should also match, so that I will not face bankruptcy as long as I can service my debt. I may face a liquidity problem if my assets cannot be cashed quickly or without a hefty loss. Solvency problems are thus different from liquidity problems. They are systemic while liquidity problems arise from portfolio choices.

A high and rising stock/flow ratio indicates a stock disequilibrium. Keynes's theory abstracted from such issues of stocks. His concern was with flow equilibrium. The flow of savings must match a flow of investment high enough to generate full employment for a Keynesian equilibrium. Yet you could have full employment and Keynesian flow equilibrium while debts are rising, as was the case during the first decade of the twenty-first century. The US was running a double deficit on its trade and budget accounts while enjoying a boom. The UK was also borrowing during the upswing on the ground that it was investment. Sadly the borrowings did not fructify into extra income and hence both economies had a stock disequilibrium.

In addition to the issue of a stock disequilibrium which the Keynesian model is not concerned with, there are also other questions related to the perception of public debt among the advocates of a Keynesian policy. Public debt does not figure as a constraint on public spending in the Keynesian view because of the notion that public debt is what the economy owes to itself. The rentiers who hold the debt can be squeezed to accept very low interest rates. The threat to the economy comes from over-saving and the rentiers do not perform a useful function. Keynesians believe that any addition to debt would be self-liquidating. Adding to the debt would lead to an increase in income that would in turn help service the debt. Debt would not matter.

Consequently, Keynesians believe that public debt is an intragenerational distribution issue. One part of society has claims on the rest that will be dealt with out of current income as and when. The debtors, by definition the majority of the citizens, can always choose to inflate the debt away or lower interest rates sufficiently to ease the burden of servicing it. Neoclassical and new classical economists, however, view public debt as an intergenerational issue. They view unpaid debt as a burden on future generations and hence a long-term liability. One factual reason for such a change of perspective may be that today we live in societies with stationary and aging populations. Also, thanks to the decades of high employment and income growth, more of us have assets on which we expect a good return. Rentiers are no longer a minority. Life expectancy is increasing and the burden of pensions and of elderly care demands more savings from all of us, as well as higher public taxes to supplement private provision. We are all rentiers now. This should make us conscious of the intergenerational burden of debt.

The lack of stocks and the closed economy vision of debt are two features which make the Keynesian model unsuitable as a guide to understanding the current crisis. In a globalized world, even the nation-state is not an autonomous borrower which can dictate its terms. The holders of the debt may be spread worldwide. Even if the debt is held by nationals, they do have the freedom to invest their money elsewhere. Since some of the rentiers may be pension funds, there is an intertemporal aspect to the necessity for the borrower to maintain a good credit rating.

The Crisis in the Eurozone

This has been shown in the eurozone crisis, which began in 2010 – the second leg of the crisis that had started with the collapse of Lehman Brothers. The European search for stability in exchange rates had climaxed in the decision to have a single currency, the euro, to which the first countries signed up in 1999.[10] The European Central Bank (ECB) was set up in the image of the German Bundesbank. It has a mandate to keep inflation low, using an explicitly monetarist strategy. The ECB cannot buy the public debt of any member country in the primary market. Thus countries cannot fund their debt by borrowing from ECB. Nor can individual countries "print" money. As they are part of a currency union, they cannot rely on depreciation of the currency to escape recession. The euro in this manner is similar to the Gold Standard, which allowed no monetary sovereignty.

The decision of a group of developed sovereign countries to revive something akin to a Gold Standard in the twenty-first century requires a bit of explanation. We have to go back to the 1970s when the old Bretton Woods arrangement of fixed exchange rates broke down. Countries were on a de facto flexible or floating exchange rate system. This was a regime for which there were no road maps. Western European countries had previously come together in an arrangement that was called the Common Market (it was later renamed the European Economic Community, EEC). France, the Federal Republic of Germany, Italy, the Netherlands, Belgium and Luxemburg were the original members of what was in effect a customs union. More countries joined the EEC so that by early 1990s there were 15 countries in the European Community/European Union, as it was now labeled. After the collapse of the Soviet Union, the

EU enlarged itself to include countries from Eastern Europe. Now there are 28 members of the EU.

The original six members of the EEC, thrown on the flexible exchange rate markets in the early 1970s, sought some arrangement – an anchor – that would provide stability. They set up a European Monetary System to facilitate cooperation among themselves, swapping currencies if necessary. Their long-run aim was "an ever closer union." Later they moved forward in an Exchange Rate Mechanism (ERM) where currencies had to maintain their level with each other within a fixed band of deviation of 2.5 percent. This was a revival of the Bretton Woods system for the small number within the EEC. The deutschmark was most often the strongest currency. It began to play the role the dollar had played in the Bretton woods system. But there was a crucial difference. The German Bundesbank had always followed orthodox monetary policy with strict control over money supply. There was no support for government debt through printing money. Germany (West Germany until the reunification in 1990) was the beacon of orthodox public finance and monetary policy. It had a sound balance of payments and a strong currency. It seemed to many European countries that they should benefit from an arrangement where the deutschmark became the anchor.

Membership of the ERM meant operating within certain rules. As in Bretton Woods, if a country's currency depreciated away from the allowed bands, deflationary policies would have to be adopted until the currency was brought back under control.

France tried a bold Keynesian experiment when François Mitterrand, the Socialist Party leader, became President in 1981. But it was quickly realized that the currency would depreciate as investors feared inflation. The expansionary policy was soon reversed and for the rest of the 1980s France followed a *franc fort* – a policy of a strong French franc.

The UK had adopted a monetarist policy after 1979. Despite a deep recession, it found the control of inflation difficult. It joined the ERM in 1989, but exited in 1992 as the pressure to maintain parity within the ERM became too costly in terms of high interest rates. The rest of the members of the ERM moved on to set up the eurozone after 2001, when the EEC had expanded and had become the EU. Nineteen countries as of now are members of the eurozone. Their woes are part of the story of the crisis as it entered its second phase.

In the first few years, the euro seemed to work fine, although the rules of fiscal discipline were not strictly adhered to, even by Germany and France. But there was a boom and countries managed to grow. They were also able to borrow on the commercial market and interest rates on sovereign debt converged to the low favorable rate Germany was paying. But once the crisis broke and liquidity became short, many eurozone countries found that the markets treated their debt as no better than that of any corporation. The yield on bonds of Greece, Italy, Spain, Ireland and Portugal went up sharply, as did credit default swaps, which were bets on likely default. Sovereign debt was no longer immune from market attack. Debt was not just an intrageneration game between citizens and rentiers, but between a country and global credit markets. Five years on, the problems facing the eurozone countries remain.

If the problem does not arise from oversaving and has no Keynesian solution, what solution can it have? Hayek had a different theory of the recession, as we have seen above. It is a Wicksellian process where mal-investments have been made during the boom, fueled by low rates of interest. Hayek had no recipe for recovery from a slump. Indeed, he was positively against reflation since he believed that the original problem had been caused by low interest rates distorting the correct gradient of prices of long-run versus short-run goods. He would recommend deleveraging until the effects of the mal-investments were worked out of the system and it started growing again.

Something of this sort seems to be the aim of UK Chancellor George Osborne's program. He has promised to cut the deficit over seven years. The Budget has been frozen in real terms at the level proposed by the previous Labour government in March of 2010, two months before the General Election. In the fourth year of austerity, the UK economy has recovered, registering a growth rate of around 2.5–3.0 percent. But it is early days yet. In the US, the political logjam with regard to the budget has led to sequestration – a de facto but arbitrary cut in public spending. This, along with an aggressive quantitative easing policy, seems to have worked. While the US is now out of recession, doubts persist about whether it will get back to the "old normal." The unemployment rate was stubbornly refusing to fall below 7 percent but in 2014 it moved significantly below 6.5 percent. GDP growth was 4.6 percent in the second quarter of 2014 and 3.6 percent in the third quarter.

The rate of inflation in developed countries is puzzling. It remains low, below the target rate given to the Central Bank. In the eurozone it is below 1 percent. This is remarkable if you think back to the 1970s when printing money was said to cause inflation. Central Banks, normally inflation hawks, are now seriously worried about the low and falling rate of inflation. They are eagerly seeking for ways of raising it. Who would have thought that possible even as recently as 2000? There are no permanent laws in economics. Only historically contingent truths.

Chapter Seven

THE SEARCH FOR AN ANSWER

We have been on a journey through the history of economic ideas. We have witnessed the strength of the equilibrium paradigm and the retreat of the only serious challenge to it by Keynes. Even Keynes was only arguing for multiple equilibria rather than a dynamic disequilibrium understanding of capitalism.

Ideas matter. They shape our understanding of the world and our search for solutions. Like the proverbial drunken man, we look for the lost keys near where the street light is. There is no guarantee that what we are looking for is anywhere near there. In looking away from where the majority look, we may make discoveries that are sometime illuminating. This is the merit of delving into the ideas of economists long neglected, those inhabiting "the underworld of economics," as Keynes said.

There is no doubt that mainstream economists did not antici-
pate the crisis and the subsequent recession. The new classical
economists do not believe such predictions are possible. The
Keynesians could have foreseen it but did not. Once it had
happened, Keynesians blamed it on the New Classicals and
advocated policies which they believed could revive the economy
quickly. Either way, all the mainstream economists have ended
up looking as though they are fighting to get seats on a train
which has already left the station.

The task now is to attempt an alternative narrative of why
things turned out the way they did. We saw in the previous
chapter what happened. Now we can ask why it happened as it
did. My explanation is built (a) on the idea of long cycles as put
forward by Kondratieff/Schumpeter, (b) supplemented by the
Marx–Goodwin notion of a cycle in the income shares of wages
and profits, and (c) the Wicksell–Hayek theory of short cycles
caused by the gap between the market rate of interest and the
natural rate. I keep the argument informal rather than mathematical, but would hope that this provides a plausible explanation of why the crisis occurred.

The Importance of the Long Perspective

Mainstream economists can argue that if a crisis occurs only
once every 70 years, their models are unlikely to predict it as
their sample often only stretches back to the postwar years. To
shed light on the occurrences and reoccurrences of crises one

would need a theory which covers a longer time span in history and might include more than just two crises. The now neglected literature on long cycles is what provides such an explanation, although in a non-rigorous way.

The severity of the present recession may be due to the confluence of a longer – Kondratieff type – cycle beginning in the 1970s along with a shorter ten-year cycle. As I explained earlier, Kondratieff cycles are not as regular as clockwork and cannot be dated precisely. They rely on a combination of longer run forces such as demographic trends and cycles, or bursts of innovation, such as the discovery of gold and silver (relevant for the Gold Standard during the nineteenth century) or innovations in credit creation, as happened in the late twentieth century, or oil/shale discoveries, and also political events which may change the geography of the markets, as the fall of the Berlin Wall did. Kondratieff did, however, cover data going back to the Industrial Revolution. The first Kondratieff cycle has an upswing from the 1780s to 1810/17 and a downward phase from 1810/17 to 1844/51.The next long cycle peaked somewhere between 1870 and 1875 and then entered a downward phase which ended in the 1890s. It is not difficult to bring these projections up to date as I did in Chapter 2 on cycles. Thus 1914/20 to 1935/40 was a downswing, while 1940/45 to 1970/75 was an upswing. The downswing then lasted from 1970/75 to 1990/95. The big upswing then was in 1990/95 to 2007/10.

Schumpeter's idea of long swings was one of bursts of innovation which happen infrequently but which each set off a long cycle of high profits, followed by imitation, which then erodes the high profits, resulting in quiescence until another cycle bursts on the scene. His research spanned the first Industrial Revolution in the eighteenth century, the revolution in transportation arising from the creation of the railroads in the first half of the nineteenth century, to innovations in electricity, telephones and automobiles in the last decade of the nineteenth century. These three innovation episodes were powerful explanators of the history of modern capitalism. Over the decades the center of gravity shifts from England to Germany and then to the US. Unfortunately, national data do not all move in harmony. To see the change in dynamics, the data of many individual countries have to be explored.

In the nineteenth and early twentieth centuries the research tradition precluded focusing on national economies. The capitalist system stretched across countries, mainly in Europe and North America, with the Antipodes added in the late nineteenth century. There was large-scale migration from Europe to North America and also to the Antipodes. Thus the demographics of the capitalist system as a whole would have to span both continents as well as Australia and New Zealand. Many economists took a European or North Atlantic view of the economic system rather than looking at individual countries.

Only since World War II have economists begun to deal with exclusively national data and economies in detail. National income data began to be estimated and published in a small way in the mid-1930s. After the war and thanks to the Keynesian revolution, national income measurement became a pivotal tool of policy-making, with ample support from governments' Treasury departments. More detailed breakdowns of expenditure and income and output developed as the years went by. Annual data were enhanced by quarterly data, and now even higher frequencies are available. This has shaped the themes and strategies of research in macroeconomics.

New classical macroeconomics has been very much concerned with analyzing US time series. Where there are multi-country models such the LINK project of Lawrence Klein, they string many individual countries together with linkages provided by exports and imports. But even so the interconnections remain weak. The older tradition had less accurate data but its vision was systemically global rather than intercountry.

The way I have interlinked the developed economies (DEs) and the emerging economies (EEs) or related the effect of Chinese growth and slowdown is not unknown. But it would be nearly impossible to build a DSGE model – of the sort the new classical economics specializes in – on this global scale. Thus we might have a discussion about the cross-country linkages at an informal, journalistic level but no attempt to weave together a systematic theoretical account.

But evidence of long cycles can still be seen in data even when we analyze single countries. Recently Thomas Piketty has analyzed the long-run trends in inequality in his book *Capital in the Twenty-First Century*. He finds evidence of long cycles of 40 to 50 years. Thus the share of labor income in Britain peaks in

1920 and again in 1970. In France the wage share exhibits a 40-year cycle with peaks in 1900, 1940 and 1980. In the US, Piketty's data show a fall in income inequality from a peak in 1940 which is regained in the mid-1990s.[1]

Given the average length of 40 to 50 years, there can only have been about four or five cycles since the Industrial Revolution. The accuracy of prediction with such a small sample is problematic. But the idea is not statistical precision (the mainstream models have plenty of that) but some intuition as to what shaped the catastrophic event.

One piece of the puzzle is provided by Marx's theory of the struggle between capital and labor for income shares which he presents in section 7 of volume 1 of *Capital*. This was the theory as expressed in mathematical terms by Richard Goodwin, as I have outlined above. For a range of parameter estimates, the model yields a long cycle prediction.[2] The key here is the wage share whose trends and cycles are the basic variable in a Marxian model. This idea needs, however, also to be extended to a global economy, although in an informal way. Let me try.

The longer cycle we have lived through can be understood through a Marxian explanation in terms of the crisis of profitability (the flip side of a rise in the share of wages). This occurred in DEs following the oil shock of the 1970s and caused the irreversible outward migration of manufacturing to the EEs. Andrew Glyn and Robert Sutcliffe explained the crisis of profitability in the DEs in terms of a rising share of wages in total income and the consequent fall in the share and the rate of profit.[3] Data gathered by the French economists Gerard Duménil and Dominique Lévy confirm the decline of profit rate in the US from a peak in the mid-1960s to a trough in 1980.[4] This outmigration of manufacturing was made possible by some recent innovations in communication such as communications satellites, computer technology, and container ships which made the shifting of entire factories from one location to another feasible. The outward migration of manufacturing began with the "mature" products, whose technology was now well known and unlikely to be changed. These factories had processes where the labor input could be easily trained to adapt and the high-wage Western labor was no longer necessary or profitable. Across DEs the share of manufacturing in total output and total employment fell.

There were other consequent changes that ensued. New jobs had to be created in the DEs and many were created in the service sector. The service sector jobs were well paid if the worker was skilled and had attained higher education. These workers got jobs in public sector education, the civil service and in private sector banking and finance. Many who were unskilled or semi-skilled and had good jobs in manufacturing were made redundant. They became the long-term unemployed or took jobs in low-paying private sector activities such as retailing or the catering trade. The extent of the split between long-term unemployment and low-paid jobs depended on how supportive the welfare state was. In Western Europe, the welfare state bore the brunt and workers stayed long-term unemployed; in the US they took low-paid jobs. In the UK data, the wage share shows a downward trend from the peak of 1975. The US data also show a similar trend, with the share of corporate income going up after the early 1980s.[5]

There was a knock-on effect on politics. Social democratic/left wing parties which relied on trade union support found that the trade unions had been weakened by their members losing their jobs and because the new service sector employees were that much more difficult to unionize. In the 1970s, the battle between Keynesians and monetarists was decisively won by the monetarists, not because the latter were necessarily right about their theories, but because they commanded greater political support. The objective of public policy became fighting inflation, with full employment a distinctly secondary goal. Central Banks gained in reputation, mainly due to the Bundesbank, which had always shunned Keynesian theories and followed a strict low-inflation policy.

The DEs responded by liberalizing their capital markets and encouraging flows overseas. This accelerated the flow of private capital, often in the shape of foreign direct investment to what came to be called the emerging economies. The emergence of China and other Asian newly industrialized countries during the subsequent decades lowered the rate of inflation in the prices of manufactured goods, which eventually led to the global imbalances. It has also slowed the growth of wage incomes in the DEs and worsened the long-run unemployment situation.

The cycle of 1970/75–1990/95 contained a Wicksellian element for the developing economies. The earnings of the oil-exporting countries could not be spent at their domestic stations. They ended up as deposits in western banks. The rate of interest was around 5 percent, way below the rate of inflation. Despite this negative real rate of interest there was no demand for bank loans in developed economies as they were going through a period of stagflation. The banks began to aggressively lend to developing economies, especially to the governments on the benign assumption that there was no such thing as sovereign default. The recipients of this largesse invested it in oil exploration, especially shale oil, ambitious real estate schemes or just gross corruption. In a way the market rate of interest was so low that almost any investment would have a higher natural rate.

This duality of a Wicksellian boom in developing countries and stagflation in developed economies prevailed through the 1970s. Toward the end of that decade, monetarists had moved into pivotal policy positions. There was to be no monetizing of public debt. Selling public debt to the market with a government determined to bring deficits down and balance the budgets meant a sharp rise in interest rates in the developed economies. This was the classic Wicksellian shock for the borrowing countries. They could not service the debt incurred at a 5 percent nominal rate when it moved into double digits. The result was a debt crisis for the developing economies, starting with Mexico in 1982. Others followed, including Nigeria, Egypt, Côte d'Ivoire, the Philippines, as well as many more. Projects had to be abandoned and mal-investments regretted in a Hayekian fashion. It took the remainder of the 1980s to unwind the debt problems of the developing economies.

The impact on the developing countries of the tightening of monetary policy by developed countries was the first instance since the late nineteenth century of a newly developing global interdependence. This was an element that had been absent in the Keynesian quarter-century 1945–70. Other such episodes were to recur till the crisis finally hit home in developed economies in the first decade of the twenty-first century.

A second cycle was set off by the collapse of the USSR and a significant acceleration in the process of globalization, which took place in the early 1990s. This was a political shock which expanded the scope of market economies. There were more forex, bonds and equity markets now for the investors to put their money into. The market economy was globalized in other ways as well. The WTO was established, capital flows to developing economies accelerated and many governments began to borrow on global financial markets. Activities on the financial front exploded as many new stock markets opened up and many new instruments were innovated: credit default swaps (CDS) and collateralized debt obligations (CDO) being lately the most notorious. Much of this was the consequence of the pioneering work of Black and Scholes on options. Hedge funds and many other institutions of what became known as the shadow banking structure also proliferated. Transactions on the forex markets reached a level of trillions of dollars. (The collapse of Long-Term Capital Management, which invested in foreign bonds, was one

THE SEARCH FOR AN ANSWER

example of the collateral damage caused by the implosion in global financial markets.)

The so-called emerging economies were able to benefit from the increased flow of foreign capital and used it to further their manufacturing industry. The WTO allowed greater exports from the EEs to the developed countries' markets. But at the same time the free flow of capital and the flexible exchange rate systems proved too risky for some EEs. A result was the Asian crisis of 1997, in which many of the EEs of Asia suffered from sudden capital outflows which emptied their forex reserves. The IMF failed to help them in a creative way. This led to the Asian economies adopting a strategy of underconsumption and over-saving, accumulating large forex surpluses.

The Asian crisis is another example of a Wicksellian boom and bust. This time the flow of capital was from investors in developed countries seeking higher returns. The recipients were lulled by techniques such as pegging the currency to the dollar, which is a way of lowering the market rate by giving the impression that exchange rate risk is zero. Once again, when inflation caused a tightening of monetary policy in the borrower countries, foreign investors moved out and caused the collapse of the currency which had hitherto been pegged. There is little evidence of any learning from past mistakes. Each generation seems to believe, especially when they are in the midst of a bubble, that the truths learnt in the past are now irrelevant: that the "paradigm" has changed or that there are better techniques available to avoid past mistakes, or as Reinhart and Rogoff indicated in the title of their opus, "This Time Is Different."[6] What was learnt after the event was that the EEs began to be mercantilist and began oversaving, putting their money in safe US T bills.

The counterpart of this oversaving was the long boom in DEs which lasted from 1992 to 2007 (with a short setback during the collapse of the dot.com boom). The boom intensified after the Asian economies began to oversave and lend their surpluses cheaply to the developed economies. This long period of 1991 to 2007 was the time during which overconsumption in the latter became the norm. This dual matching of Western over-consumption and Asian underconsumption fed a debt-fueled boom in the developed countries, with households in the devel-oped economies undersaving. An additional cause of the persist-ence of such undersaving was the sophistication of financial markets, which were able to build ever taller inverted pyramids of debt on a small base of cash. When the bubble burst, it was a double crisis of insolvency and illiquidity for the banks and other financial intermediaries.

This long boom in the developed economies was the third example of a Wicksellian cycle intertwining with the longer Kondratieff cycle. The contours were remarkably similar to what happened to the developing countries in the 1970s when the flood of oil export revenues was deposited in Western banks. This time it was the Asian countries' export surpluses which were the trigger, and putting them in T bills produced the exact same effect. Developed economies prided themselves on the sophistication of their hedging techniques and the smartness of their portfolio managers. But the bottom line was that they were all behaving like the Gadarene swine, blindly following the leader to their destruction. There was euphoria and positive correlation rather than risk aversion and diversification. Only the amounts lost were much larger than in the 1970s.

For the developed countries the share of wages peaked in the early 1970s. The decline, though, has not been reversed even after 40 years. The shift in manufacturing to the developing economies meant the end of guaranteed high and rising real wage employment for unskilled and semiskilled manual workers. In the developing economies, however, there is little evidence of any pressure on wages as a result of the rise of manufacturing exports. There has been a rise in per capita income in most of the Asian economies but the wage share has been at best not deteriorating.

Thomas Piketty's data confirm this trend. It was promoted through capital market liberalization and the growth of financial markets with sophisticated innovations. Incomes of the majority of workers in the US stagnated. When the financial markets provided cheap borrowing through issuing credit cards, mortgages and other schemes, workers took advantage. They maintained high consumption levels even though they were building up debt. At the same time governments carried on borrowing even in prosperous times. Apart from the two last years of the Clinton Administration, the US Budget has been in deficit from the time Reagan became President. During the presidency of

George W. Bush (2001–9), the US ran a trade deficit in addition to the budget deficit. The defense was that given the savings glut, America was doing a noble job by being the consumer of the last resort. But it also became a debtor of the first rank.

The long boom of 1945–70 was based on a demographic surge and the growth of manufacturing which held up workers' income. Governments had stable tax revenue and savings in pension contribution from people working their way for a few more decades before they were to retire. There was investment in many innovations which had been made during the war and soon after. Government budgets were more or less in balance despite the built-in stabilizers. The second boom of 1992–2007 was very different. Workers' incomes were flat, if not falling. There was an aging population and pension funds were under pressure. Households in developed economies ceased to save. Financial services became a large and vital part of the economy, exceeding the manufacturing sector in size in many countries. There were few productive investment opportunities left. Consumption helped shore up the economic growth but was fueled by credit.

In a new classical macro model, none of these many distinctions matters. The economy produces a single good and all workers get employed as long as they negotiate a money wage which suits them. Unemployment is voluntary. The composition of output – manufacturing or services – does not matter. The deficits on budget and trade also do not affect the workings of the model. There is just one financial asset, a bond. It is no wonder that the models failed to pick up the signals of weakness in the global economy.

The alternative explanation I have advanced in terms of a dynamic disequilibrium model of capitalism, using the ideas of Marx, Schumpeter, Wicksell and Hayek, has the merit of being able to weave together a global story with real and financial factors interplaying their roles against a background of political changes. Demographic factors also come into play differently in the first Keynesian boom of 1945–70 as compared to the later boom of 1992–2007. It would be a challenge to build a formal econometric model which can encompass these elements but it is not impossible. We have techniques of time series analysis which have rigorous ways of separating trends and cycles, and some which can pinpoint the frequency at which the maximum variability in the data is concentrated. Thus to spot a four- or ten-year cycle in the data or to locate whether a longer 40- or 50-year cycle can explain variability in the data is not beyond our statistical toolkit.

Is the Future Bleak?

If there is some validity to my hypothesis, we should be now in a downward phase of a Kondratieff which may last anything up to 20 to 25 years. We already have worries about the declining rate of inflation and growth stagnation in the eurozone area. Growth in China is slowing down, albeit only to 7 percent. It is unlikely that economies that have recovered, such as the US and UK, will get back to the old growth rate of 1992–2007. The "new normal" will be slower growth, though perhaps with falling rather than rising prices. The global economy has been in such a situation before, during the long cycle of 1873–96. It is not a circle but a spiral that the global economy is currently traversing. There will continue to be crises and cycles while capitalism is with us, which may be for long time.

As the crisis in the developed economies continues, the best that is on offer is a slow recovery; the high growth rates of 1992–2007 are not likely to return anytime soon. Indeed the fashionable talk is of "secular stagnation," led by Larry Summers, sometime Harvard professor and president, Treasury Secretary and a senior advisor to President Obama.[7] This was also the pessimistic prediction of Alvin Hansen, the American proselytizer of Keynes. Hansen argued in the immediate postwar years that the US would be trapped in a secular stagnation. This was because he shared Keynes's idea that there would be oversaving and few investment opportunities for a rich country. He had also taken an interest in Kondratieff cycles and surmised that the US would be in the downswing of a Kondratieff cycle.

As it happened, he was completely wrong. The Kondratieff downswing was dated to be between 1914 and 1940 and the upswing from 1940/45 onwards. This illustrates that predictions based on Kondratieff cycles have to be treated with due caution. But if we persist in this direction, there is substance to the pessimism. The Kondratieff upswing must have spent itself between 1990/95 and 2007/10. As Kondratieff waves go, this is a short upswing. Previously the upswing from 1890/96 onward ended with World War I in 1914 for Europe, though it continued for the US. The financial crash of 2008 was unprecedented and has to be cited as the one reason why the upswing was cut short.

But if the upswing ended sooner than expected, we may have to conjecture that we are now in a long downswing. Secular stagnation is here. To explore its likely effects we could go back to a previous Kondratieff downswing of the late nineteenth century. This lasted from 1870/75 to 1890/96. Prices fell steadily during this period due to a transport revolution which brought commodities from the Antipodes to Europe and also improved technology in manufacturing. Prices fell annually by 1.7 percent between 1873 and 1882 and by 0.9 percent between 1882 and 1889, stayed level for the next ten years and only began to rise during the upswing of 1890/96–1914/20. There are already concerns about the low level of inflation in the eurozone as well as in the US and UK. The new danger is labeled "stag-deflation," which combines unemployment with low or negative rates of inflation. Could the global economy repeat the nineteenth century's experience of the Great Depression of 1873–96?

Again the long downswing of 1873–96 cautions against any quick judgment. While prices were on a downswing, income growth in the UK remained positive throughout the cycle. Income growth was 1.68% per annum for 1874–83, 1.55% for 1883–9, 2.19% for 1889–99, 1.35% for 1899–1907 and 1.72% for 1907–13. Thus the so called "Long Depression" was a depression in prices, not in real income. Can we expect such a benevolent outcome in the twenty-first century or are we doomed to have stag-deflation, as the new name goes for the malaise that afflicts us?

There are several qualifications to be entered into this simplistic view. For one thing, the global economy has many more growth poles than it had when only the developed countries were the focus of the study of cycles. The EEs are still growing at a respectable pace – China at 7 percent. India has slowdown in growth but is expected to bounce back to its previous rate of around 7–8 percent and may grow even faster if it uses its demographic dividend. Indonesia, Vietnam, Mexico and Malaysia are all still growing strongly. In the first decade of the twenty-first century, sub-Saharan Africa has seen many economies growing at a good rate. Nigeria, Ghana, Kenya, Mozambique and Mauritius are averaging 5 percent per annum. There is a lot of potential there.

The EEs save a lot and invest a lot.[8] Some like China oversave. But even in China the seeds of change are being sown and recently there has been a refashioning of economic policy that could shift the emphasis away from exports toward domestic consumption. While China needs to save less, the DEs need to save more. The EEs have proved to be highly productive as manufacturers and continue to lower prices. They consistently out compete the DEs for markets in an increasingly large number of areas. The population is large and (except for China) is growing in most EE nations. Two-thirds of India's 1.2 billion people are under 35 years.

Even so, in terms of the GDP, the developed economies still predominate and the growth of EEs does not fill the gap between total savings and investment opportunities. One thing is most likely. Growth rates of GDP will be lower than during the previous boom. The population is stagnant and aging in most DEs except for the US. In the US, the population is likely to increase from 300 million to over 400 million by the end of the century. Over the 150 years from 1950 to 2100 it would have doubled. Europe's population, by contrast, is likely to go up from around 500 million in 1950 to just about 700 million in 2100. Many European nations have less than the required rate of demographic growth for a constant population. The UK is an exception, with the birth rate exceeding the net reproduction rate. This has been attributed to the migration rates to the UK. Europe has an aging population, with the proportion aged 64 and above (16.4 percent) exceeding those aged 0 to 15 (15.3 percent). The median age in European countries (39.9) is higher than in all other countries except Japan. Migration from the EEs to the DEs may ease the burden of looking after an aging population. Yet as of now immigration is a politically explosive topic in Europe. This has been partly due to the problems of assimilation of peoples from different cultures and partly because during the recent recession public opinion has begun to scapegoat immigrants for what are larger macroeconomic difficulties.

In the eighteenth century, Adam Smith provided a definitive answer to the hotly debated question: Where does growth come from? He showed that the best source of national growth was the productivity of a country's workers. When growth seemed automatic, it was easy to put faith in steady technical progress, as

Robert Solow did in his pioneering work. But what the world needs now is another bout of Schumpeterian innovations. Only this can transform the prospects for the DEs and the world. But whether companies will want to innovate when prices are falling is a question that needs to be addressed.

There has been a continuing revolution in communications technology ever since the Silicon Valley boom began in the 1980s. We have moved from computers that occupied entire rooms to desktops and laptops, and now on to tablets. Emailing has changed office routine as well as interpersonal communications. The office can in principle be location free. There are many ways of downloading movies and music on to your devices. This technology has affected record companies, newspapers and TV channels. Universities are under pressure because thousands of students can register for online courses offered by distinguished teachers for free. New innovations in payment methods have become possible which will change the way we use banks. On the industrial side we have 3D printing and robotics that may yet revolutionize manufacturing. There are advances in DNA mapping and its effects on health may be enormous.

Innovations in technology have a displacement effect. Such was the case with the plight of Silesian weavers that concerned Marx. In the last few decades we have seen the recent shift of manufacturing to the East and the replacement of routine labor as a result of technological advances. The issue will be where the jobs can come from to employ the people coming on to the job market. There is more change ahead as we face the next generation of the shift of manufacturing away from the West as the EEs move into high tech manufacturing and match the range of goods that have previously been the preserve of developed economies. Yet if manufacturing jobs will be subject to competition, there will be a need for skilled people to do what one may call one-to-one jobs. We will need carers for the elderly, personal fitness advisors or financial advisors to take care of our affairs. Will there be enough jobs?

We have lived through previous technological revolutions. Some of us have transited through at least two if not three such revolutions within a lifetime. My formative years were spent in India. At that time most households did not have a telephone; arrangements and plans were made in person or by post. That remained the case even when I arrived in London in the mid-1960s. In India, we had a radio, which was then a rarity for a household to own. There were gramophones with needles to play 78 rpm vinyl records, but they were a luxury item for most households. Now we have gone beyond cassettes and CDs to downloading content to smartphones. I have more than one mobile telephone, a landline, TV, and many radios. Better quality mobile phones replace many of the tools we used to have: pocket diaries, calculators, cameras.

I did not fly till I was 21 and have not stopped flying frequently since. The planes have become faster, bigger and more spacious. The first computer I used during my graduate studies had been built for World War II – the UNIVAC 1. We had a turnaround time of 24 hours, which we thought was fast. Now my mobile phone has more power than the UNIVAC had and I can do my computing wherever I wish. Living in Baroda, a city in Gujarat, even South Indian cuisine was exotic. Now I can sample the cuisine of any of the hundred countries whose cooks and restaurants tickle my palate in London. So there is no reason why people younger than me should not have the same surprises, opportunities and problems as I had. The world should continue to be a better place, economically at least. We just don't know what is around the corner today, anymore than we knew when the CD threatened to displace the 33 rpm records and we thought that was a great loss.

With each innovation some jobs disappeared but others took their place. Railroads replaced stagecoaches and cars replaced railroads in many countries. The jobs lost for stagecoach drivers were regained by railroad workers, and later railroad jobs were replaced by car factory workers, gas station attendants and motorway cafés. Each technology has its own special skill set and creates opportunities for employment. There are fewer letters to post but 20 or more emails for each letter not written. The labor force engaged in internet-related activities could not have been imagined 30 years ago. A generation of trade unionists believed that computers would replace human labor. But while some labor became redundant, other jobs were created to take their place.

The world's population has grown fastest during the last century from less than 2 billion in 1900 to more than 6 billion now. The world's per capita income is higher in 2014 than it was in 1914. In Asia and Africa per capita incomes in most if not all countries are higher today than they were 50 or 100 years ago. Through the ups and downs of Kondratieff cycles, more people have been taken out of absolute poverty in Asia than was ever thought possible. Much remains to be done but it cannot be denied that in many instances reality has surpassed our imaginations. There is inequality of income and wealth and in many countries it is increasing. Yet inequality of income as between nations has come down. This is why emerging economies stand much taller today than they did 50 years ago.

This, one may say, is the fascination and horror of capitalism. It destroys jobs and creates new ones. It uproots communities and puts in their place new ones. The economic map of the world is constantly moving as far as its center of gravity is concerned. It happened half a millennium ago when the Iberian sailors discovered the New World and the East Indies, and when the most economically powerful nations were China and India. Trade between the West and Asia always ran a balance in favor of Asia, which massed the gold which had come to Europe via the New World. Then in the mid-eighteenth century the first cluster of innovations occurred which shifted the center of gravity violently away from the East and made the West the master. Western empires conquered Asia and Africa.

The next few clusters of technological innovations occurred in the West and capitalism was transformed into a world system. The balance shifted from Europe to North America at the beginning of the twentieth century. In the remainder of the twentieth century capitalism encountered many challenges, especially when the Soviet Union created a rival economic system. Colonies became independent of their imperial masters after World War II. The Cold War lasted nearly 50 years

The innovations kept on coming. After 1945 the developed countries had witnessed the first decades of mass prosperity. The idea that any economy could pursue development and pull its people out of poverty became commonplace. Japan emerged from its defeat to become a technological pioneer and leapt into the ranks of developed economies. It was the first Asian country to do so. At the end of the Cold War capitalism regained its global scope, and the next set of transformations took place which could not have been anticipated. It was the Asian countries, long called backward or underdeveloped, which emerged center stage – China and the Asian Tigers. Now it may be the turn of African countries.

Capitalism is a dynamic system but it works through creating cycles and crises. It is a disequilibrium system. Its fruits are plenty but they are not always distributed evenly or to the old elites. New fortunes are created constantly as old ones are destroyed. The death of capitalism has been foretold many times and yet it lives on. That perhaps may be the only certainty that we can all rely on.

Karl Marx, that eternal optimist, once wrote:

No social order is ever destroyed before all the productive forces for which it is sufficient have been developed and new superior relations of productions never replace older ones before the material conditions for their existence have matured within the framework of the old society. Mankind thus inevitably sets itself only such tasks as it is able to solve, since closer examination will always show that the problem arises only when the material conditions for its solution are already present or at least in the course of formation.[9]

Perhaps he was right on this one observation. We shall solve the problems yet. No one can say just how.

NOTES

Introduction: Unraveling the Threads

1. The definition is from Raymond Goldsmith, "Comment on Hyman P. Minsky, 'The Financial Instability Hypothesis,'" in C. P. Kindleberger and J. P. Lafargue, eds, *Financial Crises: Theory, History and Policy* (Cambridge University Press, Cambridge, 1982), p. 42.
2. See Timothy Geithner, *Stress Test: Reflections on Financial Crises* (Random House Business Books, London, 2014).
3. Raghuram Rajan, "Has Financial Development Made the World Riskier?" NBER Working Paper No. 11728 (National Bureau of Economic Research, Cambridge, MA, 2005); and his *Fault Lines: How Hidden Fractures Still Threaten the World Economy* (Princeton University Press, Princeton, NJ, 2010).
4. Robert Lucas, "In Defence of the Dismal Science," *The Economist*, August 6, 2009.
5. I have dealt with the theories of Marx and Hayek in Meghnad Desai, *Marx's Revenge: The Resurgence of Capitalism and the Death of Statist Socialism* (Verso, London, 2002).
6. Lord Overstone, "Reflections Suggested by a Perusal of Mr. J. Horsley Palmer's Pamphlet on the Causes and Consequences of the Pressure on the Money Market," 1837.

1 The Building Blocks

1. Earl J. Hamilton, *War and Prices in Spain 1651–1800* (Russell & Russell, New York, 1969).
2. Adam Smith, *The Theory of Moral Sentiments* (1759), ed. D. D. Raphael and A. L. Macfie (University of Glasgow Press, Glasgow, 1976), pp. 380–1.

3. J. M. Keynes, *The General Theory of Employment, Interest and Money* (1936), in *The Collected Writings of John Maynard Keynes*, vol. 7 (Macmillan, London, 1978), pp. 32–3.

2 Cycles for the Curious

1. Henry Thornton, *An Enquiry into the Nature and Effects of the Paper Credit of Great Britain* (1802), ed. F. A. Hayek (Allen & Unwin, London, 1939), ch. 3.
2. Thomas Attwood, Evidence to the Committee on the Bank of England Charter, August 2, 1832, in *Selection of Reports and Papers of the House of Commons: Banking – Currency*, vol. 30 (House of Commons, 1832), p. 467, para. 5758.
3. Meghnad Desai, *Marx's Revenge: The Resurgence of Capitalism and the Death of Statist Socialism* (Verso, London, 2002).
4. Karl Marx and Friedrich Engels, *The Communist Manifesto* (1848), ed. Gareth Stedman Jones (Penguin Classics, London, 2002), pp. 225–6.
5. Karl Marx and Frederick Engels, *Collected Works* (Lawrence & Wishart, London, 1975–2004), vol. 6, pp. 307–8.
6. Karl Marx, *Capital*, vol. 1: *Capitalist Production* (1867), trans. Samuel Moore and Edward Aveling (Swan Sonnenschein, Lowry, London, 1887), Part 7.
7. Knut Wicksell, *Interest and Prices* (1898), trans. from the German by R. F. Kahn (Macmillan, London, 1936).
8. For Kondratieff, see J. Eatwell, M. Millgate, and P. Newman, eds, *The New Palgrave Dictionary of Economics* (Macmillan, London, 1987).

3 New Tools for a New Profession

1. For Irving Fisher and the quantity theory of money, see Meghnad Desai, *Testing Monetarism* (Pinter, London, 1981).
2. Pigou's money demand equation is discussed in Desai, *Testing Monetarism*.
3. Arthur C. Pigou, *The Economics of Welfare* (Macmillan, London, 1920).
4. J. M. Keynes, *The Economic Consequences of the Peace* (1919), in *The Collected Writings of John Maynard Keynes*, vol. 2 (Macmillan, London, 1971), pp. 6–7.
5. For Cassel's PPP theory and the debate in the UK, see Desai, *Testing Monetarism*, pp. 193–5.
6. For the Cobb-Douglas production function and Paul Douglas, see J. Eatwell, M. Millgate, and P. Newman, eds, *The New Palgrave Dictionary of Economics* (Macmillan, London, 1987).
7. For Mitchell and Kitchin, see Eatwell et al., *The New Palgrave Dictionary of Economics*.
8. Eugen Slutsky, "The Summation of Random Causes as the Source of Cyclical Processes" (1927), trans. from the Russian, *Econometrica*, 6.5 (April 1937).
9. Ragnar Frisch., "Propagation Problems and Impulse Problems in Dynamic Economics," in K. Koch, ed., *Economic Essays in Honour of Gustav Cassel* (George Allen & Unwin, London, 1933).

4 Causing a Stir

1. See J. M. Keynes, *The Collected Writings of John Maynard Keynes*, vol. 13 (Macmillan, London, 1973).

2. J. M. Keynes, *The General Theory of Employment, Interest and Money* (1936), in *The Collected Writings of John Maynard Keynes*, vol. 7 (Macmillan, London, 1978), p. 203.
3. Paul A. Samuelson, "Interaction between the Multiplier Analysis and the Accelerator Principle," *Review of Economics and Statistics*, 21.2 (1939): 75–8.
4. Arthur C. Pigou, "The Classical Stationary State," *Economic Journal*, 37.212 (1943): 343–51.
5. John R. Hicks, "Mr. Keynes and the 'Classics': A Suggested Interpretation," *Econometrica*, 5 (1937): 147–59.
6. Roy Harrod, *Towards a Dynamic Economics* (Macmillan, London, 1948).
7. Martin Bronfenbrenner, ed., *Is the Business Cycle Obsolete?* (Wiley, New York, 1970).
8. What he actually said was "Indeed let us be frank about it – most of our people have never had it so good."
9. Chamberlain's economic policy is discussed in Nick Smart, *Neville Chamberlain* (Routledge, London, 2010), ch. 9.
10. See Lawrence R. Klein, *Economic Fluctuations in the United States, 1921–1941* (Wiley, New York, 1950); Lawrence R. Klein and Arthur S. Goldberger, *An Econometric Model of the United States 1929–1952* (Wiley, New York, 1955).
11. Frank Adelman and Irma Adelman, "The Dynamic Properties of the Klein-Goldberger Model," *Econometrica*, 27 (Oct. 1959): 596–625.
12. J. M. Keynes, *The General Theory of Employment, Interest and Money* (1936), p. 289.
13. Milton Friedman. and David Meiselman, "The Relative Stability of Monetary Velocity and the Investment Multiplier in the United States 1897–1958," in *Stabilization Policies*, a series of research studies for the Commission on Money and Credit (Prentice-Hall, Englewood Cliffs, NJ, 1963).
14. The debate between Friedman-Meiselman and their Keynesian rivals is described in Meghnad Desai, *Testing Monetarism* (Pinter, London, 1981).
15. A. W. H. Phillips, "The Relationship between Unemployment and the Rate of Change of Money Wage Rates in the United Kingdom, 1861–1957," *Economica*, ns, 25.100 (1958): 283–99.
16. Paul A. Samuelson and Robert Solow, "Analytical Aspects of an Anti-Inflation Policy," *American Economic Review*, 50.2, Papers and Proceedings (May 1960).
17. The argument is explained in Desai, *Testing Monetarism*, pp. 68–72.
18. Milton Friedman, "The Role of Monetary Policy," *American Economic Review*, 58.1 (Mar. 1968): 1–17.

5 Declining Fortunes

1. Ernest Mandel, "The Economics of Neo-Capitalism," in R. Miliband and J. Saville, eds, *The Socialist Register 1964* (Monthly Review Press, New York, 1964).
2. Andrew Glyn and Robert Sutcliffe, "The Collapse of UK Profits," *New Left Review*, 66 (Mar.–Apr. 1971).
3. Richard Goodwin, "A Growth Cycle," in C. H. Feinstein, ed., *Capitalism, Socialism and Economic Development: Essays in Honour of Maurice Dobb* (Cambridge University Press, Cambridge, 1967). See also Meghnad Desai, "Growth Cycles

and Inflation in a Model of the Class Struggle," *Journal of Economic Theory* (Dec. 1973), republished in *The Selected Essays of Meghnad Desai*, vol. 1: *Macroeconomics and Monetary Theory* (Edward Elgar, Cheltenham, 1995).

4. For a comparison of Hayek and Marx, see Meghnad Desai, "Hayek and Marx," in E. Feser, ed., *The Cambridge Companion to Hayek* (Cambridge University Press, Cambridge, 2006).

5. Robert Lucas, "Econometric Testing of the Natural Rate Hypothesis," in O. Eckstein, ed., *The Econometrics of Price Determination* (Board of Governors of the Federal Reserve System, Washington, DC, 1972).

6. F. A. Hayek, "Economics and Knowledge," *Economica*, 4.13 (Feb. 1937): 33–54.

7. Robert Lucas, "Econometric Policy Evaluation: A Critique," in K. Brunner and A. Metzler, eds, *Carnegie-Rochester Conference Series on Public Policy*, 1.1 (1976): 19–46.

8. See, for instance, Frank Smets and Raf Wouters, *An Estimated Stochastic Dynamic General Equilibrium Model of the Euro Area*, ECB Working Paper 171 (European Central Bank, Frankfurt, 2002).

9. Fisher Black and Myron Scholes, "The Pricing of Options and Corporate Liabilities," *Journal of Political Economy*, 81.3 (May–June 1973): 637–54.

6 The New Globalization

1. For some historical background, see Meghnad Desai, *Marx's Revenge: The Resurgence of Capitalism and the Death of Statist Socialism* (Verso, London, 2002).

2. For background on the Asian crisis see Julia Leung, *The Tides of Capital: How Asia Surmounted the Crisis and Is Now Guiding World Recovery* (Official Monetary and Financial Institutions Forum, London, 2015).

3. See Roger Lowenstein, *When Genius Failed: Rise and Fall of Long Term Capital Management* (Fourth Estate, New York, 2002).

4. J. M. Keynes, *The General Theory of Employment, Interest and Money* (1936), in *The Collected Writings of John Maynard Keynes*, vol. 7 (Macmillan, London, 1978), pp. 158–9.

5. Many books describe and analyze the crisis in detail. See Andrew Ross Sorkin, *Too Big to Fail* (Viking, New York, 2009); Raghuram Rajan, *Fault Lines: How Hidden Fractures Still Threaten the World Economy* (Princeton University Press, Princeton, NJ, 2010).

6. Alan Greenspan's testimony to the Senate Committee on Oversight and Government Reform, US House of Representatives, October 23, 2008. See also Alan Greenspan, *The Age of Turbulence*, with a new epilogue (Penguin, New York, 2008).

7. Financial Services Authority, *The Turner Review: A Regulatory Response to the Global Banking Crisis* (Financial Services Authority, London, 2009), p. 39.

8. The case for the Keynesians is argued by Robert Skidelsky, *Keynes: The Return of the Master* (Penguin, London, 2009).

9. Milton Friedman and Anna Schwartz, *A Monetary History of the United States 1867–1960* (Princeton University Press, Princeton, NJ, 1963).

10. For the background to the euro, see David Marsh, *The Euro: The Battle for the New Global Currency* (Yale University Press, New Haven, CT, 2009).

7 The Search for an Answer

1. Thomas Piketty, *Capital in the Twenty-First Century* (Belknap Press, Cambridge, MA, 2014), see figure 6.1, p. 200; figure 6.2, p. 201; figure 8.5, p. 291.

2. Meghnad Desai, "An Econometric Model of the Share of Wages in National Income: UK 1855–1965" (1984), republished in *The Selected Essays of Meghnad Desai*, vol. 1: *Macroeconomics and Monetary Theory* (Edward Elgar, Cheltenham, 1995).

3. Andrew Glyn and Robert Sutcliffe, "The Collapse of UK Profits," *New Left Review*, 66 (Mar.–Apr. 1971).

4. Gerard Duménil and Dominique Lévy, "The Crisis of the Early 21st Century: Marxian Perspectives," in R. Bellofiore and G. Vertova, eds, *The Great Recession and the Contradictions of Contemporary Capitalism* (Edward Elgar, Cheltenham, 2014).

5. Piketty, *Capital in the Twenty-First Century*, ch. 5.

6. Carmen M. Reinhart and Kenneth S. Rogoff, *This Time Is Different: Eight Centuries of Financial Folly* (Princeton University Press, Princeton, NJ, 2009).

7. Lawrence Summers, "Why Stagnation May Prove to Be the New Normal," *Financial Times*, Dec. 15, 2013.

8. Julia Leung, *The Tides of Capital: How Asia Surmounted the Crisis and Is Now Guiding World Recovery* (Official Monetary and Financial Institutions Forum, London, 2015).

9. Karl Marx, Preface to *A Contribution to the Critique of Political Economy* (1859), trans. S. W. Ryazanskaya, ed. Maurice Dobb (Lawrence & Wishart, London, 1971), p. 21.

BIBLIOGRAPHY

Adelman, F. and I. Adelman, "The Dynamic Properties of the Klein-Goldberger Model," *Econometrica*, 27 (Oct. 1959): 596–625.

Attwood, T., Evidence to the Committee on the Bank of England Charter, August 2, 1832. In *Selection of Reports and Papers of the House of Commons: Banking – Currency*, vol. 30, p. 467, para. 5758. House of Commons, 1832.

Aubrey, T., *Profiting from Monetary Policy: Investing through the Business Cycle*. Palgrave Macmillan, London, 2013.

Bellofiore, R. and G. Vertova, eds, *The Great Recession and the Contradictions of Contemporary Capitalism*. Edward Elgar, Cheltenham, 2014.

Black, F. and M. Scholes, "The Pricing of Options and Corporate Liabilities," *Journal of Political Economy*, 81.3 (May–June 1973): 637–54.

Bronfenbrenner, M., ed., *Is the Business Cycle Obsolete?* Wiley, New York, 1970.

Corry, B., *Money, Saving and Investment in English Economics 1800–1850*. Macmillan, London, 1962.

Crosland, C. A. R., *The Future of Socialism*. Jonathan Cape, London, 1956.

Darling, A., *Back from the Brink: 1000 Days at Number 11*. Atlantic Books, London, 2011.

Desai, M., "Hayek and Marx." In E. Feser, ed., *The Cambridge Companion to Hayek*. Cambridge University Press, Cambridge, 2006.

Desai, M., "Hayek: Another Perspective." In R. Skidelsky, ed., *The Economic Crisis and the State of Economics*. Centre for Global Studies, London, 2009.

Desai, M., "Keynesianism Isn't Working," *Guardian*, Feb. 16, 2009.

Desai, M., *Marx's Revenge: The Resurgence of Capitalism and the Death of Statist Socialism*. Verso, London, 2002.

Desai, M., "Saving Capitalism from Its Friends," *Guardian*, Sept. 19, 2008.

Desai, M., *The Selected Essays of Meghnad Desai*, vol. 1: *Macroeconomics and Monetary Theory*. Edward Elgar, Cheltenham, 1995.

Desai, M., *Testing Monetarism*. Pinter, London, 1981.

Desai, M., "Who'd Be a Keynesian?" *Guardian*, Oct. 22, 2008.

Desai, M. and Y. Said, eds, *Financial Crises and Global Governance*. Routledge, London, 2003.

Duesenberry, J. S., G. Fromm, L. R. Klein, and E. Kuh, eds, *The Brookings Quarterly Econometric Model of the United States*. Rand McNally, Chicago, 1965.

Duménil, G. and D. Lévy, "The Crisis of the Early 21st Century: Marxian Perspectives." In R. Bellofiore and G. Vertova, eds, *The Great Recession and the Contradictions of Contemporary Capitalism*, pp. 26–49. Edward Elgar, Cheltenham, 2014.

Eatwell, J., M. Millgate, and P. Newman, eds, *The New Palgrave Dictionary of Economics*. Macmillan, London, 1987.

Financial Services Authority, *The Turner Review: A Regulatory Response to the Global Banking Crisis*. Financial Services Authority, London, 2009.

Floud, R. and D. McCloskey, eds, *The Economic History of Modern Britain since 1700*. 2nd edn. 3 vols. Cambridge University Press, Cambridge, 1994.

Friedman M., "The Role of Monetary Policy," *American Economic Review*, 58.1 (Mar. 1968): 1–17.

Friedman, M., *A Theory of the Consumption Function*. Princeton University Press, Princeton, NJ, 1957.

Friedman, M. and D. Meiselman, "The Relative Stability of Monetary Velocity and the Investment Multiplier in the United States 1897–1958." In *Stabilization Policies*, a series of research studies for the Commission on Money and Credit. Prentice-Hall, Englewood Cliffs, NJ, 1963.

Friedman M. and A. Schwartz, *A Monetary History of the United States 1867–1960*. Princeton University Press, Princeton, NJ, 1963.

Frisch, R., "Propagation Problems and Impulse Problems in Dynamic Economics." In K. Koch, ed., *Economic Essays in Honour of Gustav Cassel*. George Allen & Unwin, London, 1933.

Galbraith, J. K., *The Affluent Society*. Houghton Mifflin, New York, 1958.

Geithner, T. F., *Stress Test: Reflections on Financial Crises*. Random House Business Books, London, 2014.

Glyn, A. and R. Sutcliffe, "The Collapse of UK Profits," *New Left Review*, 66 (Mar.–Apr. 1971).

Godwin, W., *An Enquiry Concerning Political Justice and Its Influence on General Virtue and Happiness* (1793). Penguin Classics, London, 1985.

Goodwin, R., "A Growth Cycle." In C. H. Feinstein, ed., *Capitalism, Socialism and Economic Development: Essays in Honour of Maurice Dobb*. Cambridge University Press, Cambridge, 1967.

Greenspan, A., *The Age of Turbulence*, with a new epilogue. Penguin, New York, 2008.

Hamilton, E. J., *War and Prices in Spain 1651–1800*. Russell & Russell, New York, 1969.

Harrod, R., *Towards a Dynamic Economics*. Macmillan, London, 1948.

Hayek, F. A., "Economics and Knowledge," *Economica*, 4.13 (Feb. 1937): 33–54.

Hayek, F. A., *Prices and Production*. Routledge, London, 1931.

Hicks, J. R., "Mr. Keynes and the 'Classics': A Suggested Interpretation," *Econometrica*, 5 (1937): 147–59.

Hicks, J. R., *Value and Capital* (1939). Clarendon Press, Oxford, 1945.

Hume, David, *Writings on Economics*, ed. E. Rotwein. Nelson, Edinburgh, 1955.

Keynes, J. M., *The Economic Consequences of the Peace* (1919). In *The Collected Writings of John Maynard Keynes*, vol. 2. Macmillan, London, 1971.

Keynes, J. M., *The General Theory and After*, Part I: *Preparation*. In *The Collected Writings of John Maynard Keynes*, vol. 13. Macmillan, London, 1973.

Keynes, J. M., *The General Theory of Employment, Interest and Money* (1936). In *The Collected Writings of John Maynard Keynes*, vol. 7. Macmillan, London, 1978.

Keynes J. M., *A Tract on Monetary Reform* (1923). In *The Collected Writings of John Maynard Keynes*, vol. 4. Macmillan, London, 1971.

Keynes, J. M., *The Treatise on Money* (1930). In *The Collected Writings of John Maynard Keynes*, vols 5 and 6. Macmillan, London, 1971.

Kindleberger, C. P. and J. P. Lafargue, eds, *Financial Crises: Theory, History and Policy*. Cambridge University Press, Cambridge, 1982.

Klein, L. R., *Economic Fluctuations in the United States, 1921–1941*. Wiley, New York, 1950.

Klein, L. R. and A. S. Goldberger, *An Econometric Model of the United States 1929–1952*. Wiley, New York, 1955.

Leijonhufvud, A., *Keynesian Economics and the Economics of Keynes*. Oxford University Press, New York, 1968.

Leung, J., *The Tides of Capital: How Asia Surmounted the Crisis and Is Now Guiding World Recovery*. Official Monetary and Financial Institutions Forum, London, 2015.

Locke, J., "Some Considerations of the Consequences of the Lowering of Interest and Raising the Value of Money" (1691). In *The Works of John Locke in Nine Volumes*, vol. 4. Rivington, London, 1824.

Lowenstein, R., *When Genius Failed: Rise and Fall of Long Term Capital Management*. Fourth Estate, New York, 2002.

Lucas, R., "In Defence of the Dismal Science." *The Economist*, August 6, 2009.

Lucas, R., "Econometric Policy Evaluation: A Critique." In K. Brunner and A. Metzler, eds, *Carnegie-Rochester Conference Series on Public Policy*, 1.1 (1976): 19–46.

Lucas, R., "Econometric Testing of the Natural Rate Hypothesis." In O. Eckstein, ed., *The Econometrics of Price Determination*. Board of Governors of the Federal Reserve System, Washington, DC, 1972.

Malthus, T. R., *An Essay on Population*. J. Johnson, London, 1798.

Mandel, E., "The Economics of Neo-Capitalism." In R. Miliband and J. Saville, eds, *The Socialist Register 1964*. Monthly Review Press, New York, 1964.

Marsh, D., *The Euro: The Battle for the New Global Currency*. Yale University Press, New Haven, CT, 2009.

Marshall, A., *The Principles of Economics* (1890). Macmillan, London, 1920.

Marx, K., *Capital*, vol. 1: *Capitalist Production* (1867), trans. Samuel Moore and Edward Aveling. Swan Sonnenschein, Lowry, London, 1887.

Marx, K., *A Contribution to the Critique of Political Economy* (1859), trans. S. W. Ryazanskaya, ed. Maurice Dobb. Lawrence & Wishart, London, 1971.

Marx, K. and F. Engels, *Collected Works*. 50 vols. Lawrence & Wishart, London, 1975–2004.

Marx, K. and F. Engels, *The Communist Manifesto* (1848), ed. Gareth Stedman Jones. Penguin Classics, London, 2002.

McDonald, O., *Fannie Mae & Freddie Mac: Turning the American Dream into a Nightmare*. Bloomsbury, London, 2012.

Mises, L. von, *The Theory of Money and Credit* (1912). Jonathan Cape, London, 1934.

Myrdal, G., *Monetary Equilibrium*. Hodge, London, 1939.

Overstone, Lord, "Reflections Suggested by a Perusal of Mr. J. Horsley Palmer's Pamphlet on the Causes and Consequences of the Pressure on the Money Market," 1837.

Philipson. N., *Adam Smith: An Enlightened Life*. Penguin, London, 2010.

Phillips, A. W. H., "The Relationship between Unemployment and the Rate of Change of Money Wage Rates in the United Kingdom, 1861–1957," *Economica*, ns, 25.100 (1958): 283–99.

Pigou, A. C., "The Classical Stationary State," *Economic Journal*, 37.212 (1943): 343–51.

Pigou, A. C., *The Economics of Welfare*. Macmillan, London, 1920.

Piketty, T., *Capital in the Twenty-First Century*. Belknap Press, Cambridge, MA, 2014.

Rajan, R., *Fault Lines: How Hidden Fractures Still Threaten the World Economy*. Princeton University Press, Princeton, NJ, 2010.

Rajan, R., "Has Financial Development Made the World Riskier?" NBER Working Paper No. 11728. National Bureau of Economic Research, Cambridge MA, 2005.

Reinhart, C. and K. Rogoff, *This Time Is Different: Eight Centuries of Financial Folly*. Princeton University Press, Princeton, NJ, 2009.

Ricardo, D., "On the High Price of Bullion." In *Works and Correspondence of David Ricardo*, ed. P. Sraffa, vol. 3. Cambridge University Press, Cambridge, 1951.

Samuelson, P. A., "Interaction between the Multiplier Analysis and the Accelerator Principle," *Review of Economics and Statistics*, 21.2 (1939): 75–8.

Samuelson, P. A. and R. Solow, "Analytical Aspects of an Anti-Inflation Policy," *American Economic Review*, 50.2, Papers and Proceedings (May 1960).

Schumpeter, J., *Business Cycles*. 2 vols. McGraw Hill, New York, 1939.

Schumpeter, J., *The Theory of Economic Development* (1913), trans. from the German by R. Opie. Harvard University Press, Cambridge, MA, 1934.

Skidelsky, R., *Keynes: The Return of the Master*. Penguin, London, 2009.

Slutsky, E., "The Summation of Random Causes as the Source of Cyclical Processes" (1927), trans. from the Russian, *Econometrica*, 6.5 (April 1937).

Smart, N., *Neville Chamberlain*. Routledge, London, 2010.

Smets, F. and R. Wouters, *An Estimated Stochastic Dynamic General Equilibrium Model of the Euro Area*. ECB Working Paper 171. European Central Bank, Frankfurt, 2002.

Smith, A., *An Inquiry into the Nature and Causes of the Wealth of Nations* (1776), ed. R. H. Campbell and A. S. Skinner. University of Glasgow Press, Glasgow, 1976.

Smith, A., *The Theory of Moral Sentiments* (1759), ed. D. D. Raphael and A. L. Macfie. University of Glasgow Press, Glasgow, 1976.

Solomou, S., "Economic Fluctuations 1870–1913." In R. Floud and D. McCloskey, eds, *The Economic History of Modern Britain since 1700*, 2nd edn, vol. 2: *1860–1939*. Cambridge University Press, Cambridge, 1994.

Sorkin, A. R., *Too Big to Fail*. Viking, New York, 2009.

Summers, L., "Why Stagnation May Prove to Be the New Normal," *Financial Times*, Dec. 15, 2013.

Thornton, H., *An Enquiry into the Nature and Effects of the Paper Credit of Great Britain* (1802), ed. F. A. Hayek. Allen & Unwin, London, 1939.

Walras, L., *Éléments d'économie politique pure, ou Théorie de la richesse sociale* (1874), trans. from 4th edn (1900) by William Jaffe, with annotations, as *Elements of Pure Economics*. Richard Irwin, Homewood, IL, 1954.

Wicksell, K., *Interest and Prices* (1898), trans. from the German by R. F. Kahn. Macmillan, London, 1936.

INDEX